CW01022363

IN THE WORDS OF SPARKS...
SELECTED LYRICS

First published by TamTam Books in the U.S.A. in 2013
Printed in the United States of America

TamTam Books want to thank: Lun*na Menoh, Shirley Berman, Ichiro
Shimizu, Kimley Maretzo, Jane Brown, Gilles Verlant, Sue Harris, Jonathan
Morris, Brian Gottlieb, Morrissey, Michael Bracewell, & Michael Silverblatt

Special thank you to Emmi Joutsi for additional editing, proof-reading, and
for being an all-round Sparks expert

TamTam Books is edited and published by Tosh Berman

Creative direction by Tom Recchion
Art direction & design by Mark Holley

tosh.berman@gmail.com
www.tamtambooks.com
www.tamtambooks-tosh.blogspot.com

ISBN: 978-0-9852724-0-1 or 0-9852724-0-6

Distributed by ARTBOOK/D.A.P.
155 6th Avenue, 2nd Floor
New York, NY 10013
www.Artbook.com

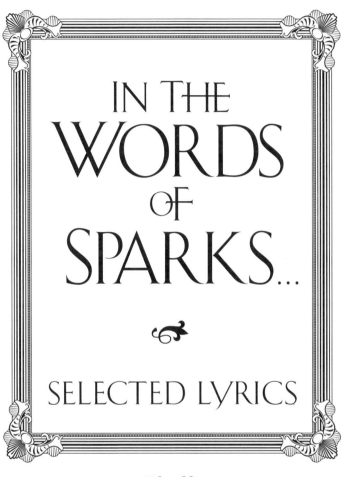

IN THE
WORDS
OF
SPARKS...

❧

SELECTED LYRICS

Edited by

RON MAEL & RUSSELL MAEL

TAM TAM
BOOKS

G D⁷ G
G D⁷ Em
D⁷ G D⁷ G (B⁷)

Repeat ↗

CHORUS
C G D G
C G D G Em

CONTENTS

Introduction by Morrissey   XI

Falling In Love With Myself Again   19
High C   21
Metaphor   22
When Do I Get To Sing "My Way"   25
In The Future   27
Madonna   30
Suburban Homeboy   32
Let's Get Funky   34
Sherlock Holmes   35
The Ghost of Liberace   37
Funny Face   39
Young Girls   41
This is the Renaissance   43
Bullet Train   45
Perfume   47
How Do I Get To Carnegie Hall?   50
Achoo   53
Whippings And Apologies   54

Without Using Hands	*56*
Rock, Rock, Rock	*58*
I Bought The Mississippi River	*61*
Those Mysteries	*63*
Girl From Germany	*65*
Popularity	*68*
Sisters	*69*
Aeroflot	*71*
Lost And Found	*73*
Change	*75*
The Rhythm Thief	*77*
Gratuitous Sax	*78*
What Are All These Bands So Angry About?	*79*
The Very Next Fight	*81*
Instant Weight Loss	*83*
My Other Voice	*85*
National Crime Awareness Week	*86*
Hear No Evil, See No Evil, Speak No Evil	*88*
Photoshop	*90*
The Louvre	*92*
Pineapple	*93*
Nothing To Do	*95*
The Wedding Of Jacqueline Kennedy To Russell Mael	*97*
Looks Aren't Everything	*98*
Over The Summer	*100*
The Number One Song In Heaven	*102*
Batteries Not Included	*104*
Looks, Looks, Looks	*105*
I Can't Believe You Would Fall For All The Crap In This Song	*109*
Live in Las Vegas	*110*

Lighten Up, Morrissey   *113*

Here Comes Bob   *115*

Propaganda   *118*

Under The Table With Her   *119*

(She Got Me) Pregnant   *120*

Tryouts For The Human Race   *124*

My Baby's Taking Me Home   *126*

When I'm With You   *128*

I've Never Been High   *130*

Pretending To Be Drunk   *131*

Equator   *132*

Tits   *134*

Ugly Guys With Beautiful Girls   *136*

I Married A Martian   *140*

I Wish I Looked A Little Better   *143*

Shopping Mall Of Love   *145*

The Toughest Girl In Town   *147*

How To Get Your Ass Kicked   *149*

This Town Ain't Big Enough For Both Of Us   *151*

Strange Animal   *153*

Mickey Mouse   *155*

Let's Go Surfing   *157*

Let The Monkey Drive   *160*

Walk Down Memory Lane   *163*

Miss The Start, Miss The End   *165*

Bon Voyage   *169*

I Thought I Told You To Wait In The Car   *171*

I Married Myself   *173*

Alphabetical Song Index   *175*

Song Copyright & Publication Information   *180*

Happy Hunting Ground
Happy Hunting Ground

who thought   I am out today
                I am out today

It's a great escape
thank you

where   I am going   I don't have a
                                care

+ All around the happy hunting ground   And I   really pity you
    the same

H

                    You shall see   Happy Hunting Ground
And the   There's a reading sound
                There's a writing sound   Happy Hunt
                There's a rithmeticing   Happy Hunting
                                                        Ground
                    For your reading

the   Happy Hunting Ground

                When you read you read from the right to left
                When you write you're missing the page
                When Your arithmatic

Happy

                I had it great
                I had thought it grand
                When they   threw me out

Happy Hunting Ground

Happy Hunting Ground
They don't tell or act like you to

Happy Hunting Ground
Happy Hunting Ground
No ~~that~~ they sure don't look like you

When you leave the
they don't

INTRODUCTION

RON AND RUSSELL MAEL always knew that what they were doing was funny.

Which is precisely why they *never* laughed.

> *"well I ain't no Freud / I'm from LA ..."*

Music hall Americana, Sparks' first and second albums composite Lear and Belloc. The desired one is always absent and life is a scattered bouquet:

> *"you've been waiting for your first encounter –*
> *what a let down / I'm just finishing my first encounter –*
> *what a let down"*

whereas their third album was pure fist-fight:

> *"you mentioned Kant and I was shocked / because where*
> *I come from none of the girls have such foul tongues"*

With a face fixed in imperishable marble, Ron Mael appears instantly as an elevated writer of inward dialogue. The human race appears to be made up of two distinct types – those who engage in the physical, and the barely sane who just don't or can't or won't. The stretcher-case aspect to Ron

Mael is magisterial shyness who nonetheless knows how the modern poet must operate.

The words do not cease to be poetry simply because music is tagged-on.

> *"cut your ties with this possessive mother – she*
> *will destroy you / cut your ties and find another one*
> *who will respect you"*

Read one way, Sparks lyrics are imperious pop; read another, they are Dali-in-motion, and a high altar of pop craft is on the move – not towards *American Bandstand*, but the hushed halls of the Smithsonian. Sparks know that the lyrics must mean something, and the private humiliation of youth finally finds its sanity when chronicled into soundscapes:

> *"it's a lot like playing the violin / you cannot start*
> *off and be Yehudi Menuhin"*

Don't underestimate the agony, but let it be soothed by public sympathy even if, at dusk and dawn, nothing spreads before you but the impatient blank page – edging you still onwards to rewrite the past as... however you'd wish it had been.

When I first heard Sparks in 1974 I had no doubt whatsoever that it mattered greatly. Strapped to a wooden bed, I was Sparks' ideal target audience. Life was not something I could recommend, but at 14 I heard *'This Town Ain't Big Enough For Both Of Us'* as Radio One's Record of the Week and I instantly rallied to champion Sparks with a heart both persecuted and puritanical. As far as my capacities would allow, I am within sight of port. That the singing voice is female is something I am as certain of as much as I can be certain of anything. I am fired. I am charged. Of course, the as-yet unbroken voice is that of Russell Mael, sounding nine-parts Saint Etienne and one part Pacific

Palisades. The shafts of satirical wit drip from brother Ron, so donnishly severe behind keyboards. Their combined sound is one previously unheard, unknown and untraceable throughout the history of recorded noise. Ron and Russell are Sparks, and if they are not Sparks they will go mad or die. Even *being* Sparks might cause them to do both. Here, though, is something sporty to do with time whilst loitering in life's waiting – room (for isn't that what life is?) Minds bent sideways, Ron and Russell glare out of television screens with looks of haunted alarm, introducing themselves to landscape Britain with their muscled poetry that works by sound, and with a certain cold-bloodedness that thankfully hoists them above the pop firmament. You will hunt long and hard to find any photographic evidence of Sparks loafing around with their contemporaries. Sparks would forever keep a distance that retains mystery; such masterly manoeuvres delicate. In 1974, Bryan Ferry (lead huntsman with Roxy Music) smirks *"No competition"* when asked about Sparks, as *'This Town Ain't Big Enough For Both Of Us'* leap-frogs to the number 2 chart position. Although their initial impact is unique and explosive, no one knows what to do with Sparks. In fact, *what are* Sparks?

Screaming teenagers confuse the pitch, and Ron returns their loving gaze with the disapproval of a science lecturer discovering smoking students playing hooky. Paul McCartney impersonates Ron's *risen-from-the-coffin* unflappability in a new video (as the influencer under the influence of the influenced) and the world turns.

> *"let's pursue this more / why would he leave so much*
> *that's warm / to his detriment / maybe he's oh so*
> *slightly bent? ask her, she would know"*

The breathless Russell delivery is difficult for the harmonizing listener to keep pace with, yet still the kids of England scream – which could hardly have been the plan?

"dear, do you often think of me / as you overlook the
sea do I qualify as dearly departed or am I /
that sucker in the sky?"

The humorously snippy exaggerations could only come from one who has dreamed away too many years – from one of a restricting television generations; of Zachary Smith's and Mr. Drysdale's – without whom there might never be *'Something For The Girl With Everything'*; yes, we're dying, but we're OK.

"well, is there anybody out there by the name of Mr. Jones?
no? Oh well I tried'

In 1976 I am blushingly photographed with Russell Mael standing outside CBGB's in New York City, the famous CBGB's canopy above our heads. I remind Russell (because he has possibly forgotten) that I had met him two years earlier in a hotel in Northenden (Manchester, England) where, once Ron and Russell had abandoned the remains of their breakfast of oranges and shortbread, my friend Hazel Bowden and I swept the droppings from their plates and kept the evidence as *have-been-was-here* data should future generations probe.

Condemned to exclusion, Sparks rightly became an enduring subject of Art. Tenacity came easily to two brothers raised in leg-irons who could only shout out via song.

"we're bored to tears until he comes /
and then we're crying because he's come"

It had always been shadow instead of sunlight, and the Maels swathed their art about them like Victorian wraps, masters of their own resources.

'no interviews, please / no interview, please /
life's not so free / for stockyard femme fatales / nor is my
life carefree and serene'

In moments of misfortune Sparks visibly rise and change, yet sexual attraction forever remains a lyrical muddle. The likelihood is that Ron's mother continued to carry him up and down the stairs, and although Russell's curls had entangled him in teen-mag novelty, Sparks were always going to count. Like landscape painters never to be pinned down, Sparks repeatedly justified themselves through the '80s and '90s in a mass of work thrown like jigsaw pieces about the sadly *not-even-skin-deep* pop whirl. Sometimes they feel as trapped as Dorothy Parker might, and occasionally we sense Edith Sitwell lashing out with her walking-stick. *The pop trap.* Still you listen and you know each song is telling you something before you realize fully what that something is. There will be no return to old terrain, and the word 'opera' applies where 'rock' never had or could or would.

Ron and Russell had always been two halves in search of a whole, and how logistically convenient to find the missing element in your own brother sitting in your own living room, watching *That Girl* on the TV. Hey presto...

> *'limited tastes / I wish I could help you a rock-headed lad /*
> *I have gotta help you'*

...and each Mael provides what the other lacks. The power of all of this is that, forty years on, questions are untouched and the riddle remains unravelled.

I am very happily content to wait further:

Morrissey

FEBRUARY 2013

Slowboat Takes me to
your home everyday—
and I wait for you
knowing you won't
come home just today
found

Slowboat sail off toward
7th sea — far away
from you but somehow
older
coming again, again
and again 'as' we mean
that from some sign it appears
you were come home Tears

Slowboat Takes me where
I'll always be
far away from you but
knowing that our won't come at
near me
you hear me
and you'll always be
a true

Just when sin was quite th
"Whats his outlet, whats
Could the gospel be h

Just what is his game
Could he be enticed
No one's quite that
No one's quite that

No More Mr. Nice Guys
Few are left but whin
No More Mr Nice Guys
Nice Guys cannot, Nice

She expressed a stro
She succeeded very we
If you had to call

He could be enticed
His game had to en
~~She's quite sorry how~~
She sees other men

No more Mr. Nice Guy
Nice guys won't suffice

Nice Guys cannot, Niz

ere's one who holds quite tight to what had worked before
is it something one can buy at some drug store
s he exercise by breaking 2 x 4's

him of his anxiety

Nice Guys cannot win.   anxiety
+ in relieving   burdens
n she's mother to quite a large, nice family
you would call it her, though she might disagree

quite nice

t, Nice Guys aren't suffice

(left) Slowboat, (right) No More Mr. Nice Guys

Falling In Love With Myself Again

Similar mother, similar father, similar dog, cat, and fish
And we'll make the same wish
When the birthday candle's lit
We'll both be older
We won't get our wish
Yes, I think that I'm falling in love with myself again

Yes, I think I'm falling in love with myself again
Yes, I think I'm falling
Yes, I think I'm falling
Yes, I think I'm falling in love with myself again

With her hand in my hand and my hand in hers
Don't we look a blur
Me and her and me and her
Hey, kiss her, oh kiss her
Our friends do concur
Yes, I think that I'm falling in love with myself again

Yes, I think I'm falling in love with myself again
Yes, I think I'm falling
Yes, I think I'm falling
Yes, I think I'm falling in love with myself again

I can't see with you in front of the mirror staring, staring
I can't hear myself think with all that music blaring, blaring

Yes, I'm falling
Falling, falling
Yes, I'm falling

Falling, falling
Yes, I think I'm falling in love with myself again
I bring home the bacon and eat it myself
Here's to my health
Hope that I am feeling well
I'm burning the candle at both ends, oh well
Yes, I think that I'm falling in love with myself again

Yes, I think I'm falling in love with myself again
Yes, I think I'm falling
Yes, I think I'm falling
Yes, I think I'm falling in love with myself again

A picket fence, well, I leaped it
Through your screen door, I've gotta meet you

High C up and High C down, down, down
Since you've left the opera, you just frown a lot
And mumble, "I'm humble."

Press clippings hang from torn wallpaper
A dust covered phone, no one would ring her

High C and High C down, down, down
Since you left the opera, you just frown a lot
And you tell me

Tell me of the time, girl, when you were so big in Vienna
And the people paid good money, yes they did, just to hear you in
your splendor

But that's all over now
But that's all over now

Limited taste, I wish I could help you
A rock-headed lad, I have got to help you

High C up and High C down, down, down
Since you left the opera you just frown a lot
And mumble, "I'm humble."

Come on home with me, girl, and we'll sing our little hearts out
We will hit High C, or maybe somewhere thereabouts

Somewhere thereabouts.

Metaphor

A metaphor is a glorious thing,
A diamond ring,
The first day of summer
A metaphor is a breath of fresh air,
A turn-on,
An aphrodisiac

Chicks dig, dig, d-i-g, dig, dig metaphors
Chicks dig, dig, d-i-g, dig, dig metaphors

Use them wisely,
Use them well,
And you'll never know the hell of loneliness

A metaphor is a popular place,
A parking space,
A multiplex showing,
A remake whose action is louder than words,
She whispers, "Can we be going, going?"

Chicks dig, dig, d-i-g, dig, dig metaphors
Chicks dig, dig, d-i-g, dig, dig metaphors

Use them wisely,
Use them well,
And you'll never know the hell of loneliness

Who's up for a metaphor?
(We're up for a metaphor)
Are you chicks up for a metaphor?
(Yes, we're up for a metaphor)

Don't, don't, don't, don't, don't mix them
(We, we, we won't mix them)

Don't, don't, don't, don't, don't mix them
(We, we, we won't mix them)
Don't, don't, don't, don't, don't mix them
(We wouldn't dream of mixing them)

Use them wisely,
Use them well,
And you'll never know the hell of loneliness

A metaphor is a glorious thing,
A diamond ring,
The first day of summer
A metaphor is a breath of fresh air,
A turn-on,
An aphrodisiac

Chicks dig, dig, d-i-g, dig, dig metaphors
Chicks dig, dig, d-i-g, dig, dig metaphors

A metaphor is a glorious thing,
A diamond ring,
The first day of summer
A metaphor is a breath of fresh air,
A turn-on,
An aphrodisiac

Chicks dig, dig, d-i-g, dig, dig metaphors
Chicks dig, dig, d-i-g, dig, dig metaphors

Use them wisely,
Use them well,
And you'll never know the hell of loneliness

A metaphor is a glorious thing
(Chicks dig, dig, d-i-g, dig, dig)
A metaphor is a breath of fresh air

(Chicks dig, dig, d-i-g, dig, dig)
A metaphor is a glorious thing
(Chicks dig, dig, d-i-g, dig, dig)
A metaphor is a breath of fresh air
(Chicks dig, dig, d-i-g, dig, dig)

Chicks dig, dig, d-i-g, dig, dig metaphors
Chicks dig, dig, d-i-g, dig, dig metaphors

Use them wisely,
Use them well,
And you'll never know the hell of loneliness

When Do I Get To Sing "My Way"

No, no use in lecturing them,
or in threatening them,
they will just say, "who are you"
Is that a question or not,
and you see that the plot
is predictable, not new
But you're still stunned at the things you will do

No, no use in taking their time,
or in wasting two dimes,
on a call to God knows who
When all you feel is the rain
and it's hard to be vain
when no person looks at you
So just be gracious and wait in the queue

So when do I get to sing "My Way"
When do I get to feel like Sinatra felt
When do I get to sing "My Way"
In heaven or hell

So when do I get to do it my way
When do I get to feel like Sid Vicious felt
When do I get to sing "My Way"
In heaven or hell

Yes, it's a tradition they say,
like a bright Christmas Day,
and traditions must go on
And though I say, yes I see,
no I really don't see,
is my smiley face still on?

Sign your name with an X, mow the lawn

So when do I get to sing "My Way"
When do I get to feel like Sinatra felt
When do I get to sing "My Way"
In heaven or hell

So when do I get to do it my way
When do I get to feel like Sid Vicious felt
When do I get to sing "My Way"
In heaven or hell

They'll introduce me.
'Hello, hello'
Women seduce me and champagne flows
Then the lights go low,
there's only one song I know

There, this home which once was serene,
now is home to the screams
and to flying plates and shoes
But I have no souvenirs
of these crackerjack years,
not a moment I could choose
And not one offer that I could refuse

So when do I get to sing "My Way"
When do I get to feel like Sinatra felt
When do I get to sing "My Way"
In heaven or hell

So when do I get to do it my way
When do I get to feel like Sid Vicious felt
When do I get to sing "My Way"
In heaven or hell

In The Future

It's winter, it's raining
You're tired, she's fainting
You're bitter, she's brooding
But don't be disenchanted
'Cause you can barely stand it

The sweep and the grandeur
The scope and the laughter
The future, the future
The future's got it covered
With what will be discovered

In the future fun is fun
(Future, future)
In the future, lots of sun
(Future, future)
I'll be there, it's up to you
(Future, future)
You'll be there if you don't do nothing foolish

You'll love it, I know it
I know what you like and
You'll love it, I know it
We'll need some vintage vino
So wash your feet and stamp away

Coming soon and everywhere
(Future, future)
Everyone will walk on air
(Future, future)
Now it seems so far away

In The Future

In The Future   we'll be smiling
                    more than

— it seems so far away   The sweetest
— stays so far away   The grandeur
                                The people

Convenience   ⭐   ~~For the future, fun is fun~~
and beauty   ~~In the future there'll be sun~~
~~won't be~~
so moody   Now it seems so far away
                         And it stays so far away
~~I know it won't be fooled~~
But
                              I can't wait
                              until it comes
                              I will share it with
⭐   someone who appreciates
"Cause   ⭐   it

And I won't be so moody
Cause every girl's a beauty

        It's Worth the wait

No slip-up

                              How bout it

                          You'll love it
        all blended   I know it
        together   I know what you like
        Convenience   and you'll love it
        and pleasure in ~~summery~~
⭐   ~~and~~ ~~weather~~ weather where So don't be
        that is better   and people   disenchanted ~~present~~
        And I won't be so moody to talk to
        Cause every girl's a beauty Your time
        ~~the~~   is on the

⭐   The only problem ever
        Is how to make it better

(Future, future)
But each day it's getting closer and closer

Convenience and pleasure
All blended together
And culture, and madness
You think you've seen it all
You've seen it all except the future

In the future...

Madonna

While the symphony played
I was starting to fade
Until I woke to a cymbal crash

I turned to my right
You were gone, that's all right
These Platonic things are a burn

I walked out on the street
While the big city lights
Tried to sell me on a way of life
That I was already living

Well, a limousine longer than
The Golden Gate Bridge
Pulled up alongside me at the curb

All the glass was blacked out
So I knew there was someone
Very important in there

Then the door opened up
And a blonde in the shadows said,
"Get inside."
And of course I got inside

Madonna, is that really you
Madonna, whatcha gonna do
Feelings, only you can have
Never, in a photograph
Feelings, only you can have

Well, she took me back to her penthouse
And showed me all her platinum records
And of course there were a lot

Then we sat on the sofa
And she turned on a classical station
But the reception was poor

And we sat there and talked
And talked a little more
And one thing led to another
As they often do in these situations

All the stars are shining tonight for me
All the stars are shining tonight, glory be

Madonna, is that really you
Madonna, whatcha gonna do
Feelings, only you can have
Never, in a photograph
Feelings, only you can have

In the morning
She fixed me a continental breakfast
And then she said, "Well, goodbye."
And I said, "Can I see you again?"
And she said, "No."
And I said, "Well, goodbye."
And I never told anyone about this
'Cause after all
It's none of their business what she or I did

Madonna, is that really you
Madonna, whatcha gonna do
Feelings, only you can have
Never, in a photograph
Feelings, only you can have

Suburban Homeboy

I am a suburban homeboy
with a suburban ho right by my side
I am a suburban homeboy and I say "yo dog"
to my pool cleaning guy
I hope I'm baggy enough for them
I play my Shaggy enough for them
I'll pop a cap up some fool at the Gap
And I'm a suburban homeboy

I am a suburban homeboy
with a suburban ho right by my side
I am a suburban homeboy
and I say "yo dog" to my detailing guy
I bought me cornrows on Amazon
I started listening to Farrakhan
My caddy and me he looks just like Jay-Z
And I'm a suburban homeboy

I am a suburban homeboy
with a suburban ho right by my side
She's known as Miss Missy Tannenbaum
and she's one freak bitch, ain't no lie
She's from the projects in St. Tropez
She looks like Iverson in a way
She yo yo's me and I yo yo her back
And I'm a suburban homeboy

She yo yo's me and I yo yo her back
And I'm a suburban homeboy
She yo yo's me and I yo yo her back
And I'm a suburban homeboy

We are suburban homeboys
With our suburban ho's right by our sides

We are suburban homeboys and we say "yo dog"
and we mean it, by God
We've got an old school mentality
Oxford and Cambridge mentality
Props to our peeps and please keep your receipts
And we are suburban homeboys
Props to our peeps and please keep your receipts
And we are suburban homeboys
Props to our peeps and please keep your receipts
And we are suburban homeboys
Props to our peeps and please keep your receipts
And we are suburban homeboys

Let's Get Funky

She arrived on a Greyhound bus
And she was young and so lean
And she smelled like a small town church
But she looked like a queen

And I walked up and asked her name
And she gave me a stare
So I said will you marry me
She just brushed at her hair

She looked hungry and knew I was
So she ate lunch with me
Then she held out a greasy hand
Rubbed the grease on my knee

Maybe she's taken a vow of silence
Maybe she's from some quiet island
Or maybe she's scared of big city life,
I don't know
Maybe she's had a difficult life
Oh c'mon baby, just a word
Just a syllable or two
Take your pick, say a word
Any word at all will do

"Let's get funky"

Sherlock Holmes

Fog matters to you and me
  But it can't touch Sherlock Holmes
Dogs bark and he knows their breed
And knows where they went last night
Knows their masters too
Oh baby, hold me tight

Just pretend I'm Sherlock Holmes
Just pretend I'm Sherlock Holmes
Just pretend I'm Sherlock Holmes

Stay, don't give me that same old act
I can call in Sherlock Holmes
He'll want your biography
And pictures of you in lace
And satin looking great
Oh baby, hold me tight

Spend the night with Sherlock Holmes
Hold me tight like Sherlock Holmes
Just pretend I'm Sherlock Holmes

Do you want to have fun
Do you want a good time
Do you want me to laugh
Do you want me to cry
Do you want me to dance
Do you want me to sing
Do you want me to joke
Should I be more like him
Oh yeah

I can dance like Sherlock Holmes
I can sing like Sherlock Holmes
But can't be Sherlock Holmes
Oh yeah

I can dance like Sherlock Holmes
I can sing like Sherlock Holmes
But can't be Sherlock Holmes

The Ghost Of Liberace

It was a dark and stormy night that I stepped out
Something strange was in the air, I couldn't figure it out
Who's there, tell me what you want from me
Oh no, I can't believe what I now see

They say the paranormal's just a sucker's game
I keep an open mind, but deep down I feel the same
Oh no, now I think I've changed my mind
Oh no, now I know I've changed my mind

The ghost of Liberace keeps on hanging 'round
Hovers over farmland, lingers over towns
The ghost of Liberace still has that mystique
If he were alive he'd now be at his peak
The ghost of Liberace
The ghost of Liberace

Across the street, in fact across the whole damn town
They're making fun of him, they try to put him down
Oh yeah, but I wished they'd let him be
Oh yeah, he's not hurting you or me

Sometimes he blinds the drivers with his shiny suits
They see that smile and they laugh at him, "hey don't shoot"
Oh no, now he's hung in effigy
On no, why can't they just let him be

The ghost of Liberace, the ghost of Liberace

The ghost of Liberace keeps on hanging 'round
Hovers over farmland, lingers over towns
The ghost of Liberace still has that mystique
If he were alive he'd now be at his peak
The ghost of Liberace
The ghost of Liberace

He hums Evita and Moon River and Michelle
Maybe that's why the people scream out "go to hell"
Oh no, now they're throwing cans of beer
Oh no, I thought ghosts could disappear

But he remains in all his glory, it's so strange
These aren't the kind of people that he can change
But wait, now they're starting to applaud
I guess there really is a God above

The ghost of Liberace keeps on hanging 'round
Hovers over farmland, lingers over towns
The ghost of Liberace still has that mystique
If he were alive he'd now be at his peak
The ghost of Liberace

Funny Face

I looked a lot like a Vogue Magazine
Perfect and smooth, they all called me a dream
Flawless and loveless, no intimacy
I only lived to be seen
Not to be touched, too clean

Funny face, I want a funny face
Funny face, I want a funny face

Billions of dollars are spent on the face
Covering, smoothing, and changing the shape
Everyone wanted a face just like mine
Nobody wanted me
Only to look like me

Funny face, I want a funny face
Funny face, I want a funny face

I'm ungrateful but I don't care
I hear comments from everywhere
Probably nothing behind the face
The face, the face

That was the day that I jumped off the bridge
Trying to end it all, I barely lived
Doctor Lamaar said, "Your face is a mess"
All of the rest you can guess

I got my one request
(He got his one request)
And I am happy, yes

(And he is happy, yes)
I got my one request
(He got his funny face)
And I am happy, yes
And I am happy, happy, happy, happy, happy

Funny face, I got my funny face
Funny face, I got my funny face

Young Girls

I like their arms
I like their legs
I like their lips
Their widening hips
Their radios

They live at home
They don't have cars
I have a home
I have a car
The like that, they like that

Young girls haven't seen the whole night
And they will hold you, though it might not be tight
And they will kiss you, though it might not be right
'Cause they are young girls

Young girls, I don't care what they say
I want to have you each and every day
I feel you, I don't care what they say
Young girls

I like their talk
Small little words
I like their style
Less of the guile
They're straight with you

Don't analyze
Don't analyze
You've seen too much
I like the touch of young girls,
Young girls

Young girls haven't seen the whole night
And they will hold you, though it might not be tight
And they will kiss you, though it might not be right
'Cause they are young girls

Young girls, I don't care what they say
I want to have you each and every day
I feel you, I don't care what they say
Young girls

This Is The Renaissance

Middle Ages sucked
Spent all day in prayer
Judgment Day was every day and
Witches burning everywhere
But now we are in luck
Beauties everywhere
Paintings filled with foxy women
No one's got a cross to bear and

This is the Renaissance
Came upon us all at once
Oh, what a renaissance
This is the Renaissance
Renaissance or Renàissance
It's still a renaissance

If you like to read
Man, you are in luck
Gutenberg is cranking out The Bible with a centerfold
So let it all hang out
No one's gonna care
Flash a little ankle and the guys will lose their self-control

'Cause, this is the Renaissance
Came upon us all at once
Oh, what a renaissance
This is the Renaissance
Renaissance or Renàissance
It's still a renaissance

Science is here
Nothing left to fear
Though the Earth is flat

It's not as flat as we feared
Music's gone wild
No Gregorian here
Contrapuntal music is the music that your parents fear

This is the Renaissance
Oh, what a renaissance
This is the Renaissance
Oh, what a renaissance

Ladies and gentlemen, boys and girls
Welcome to The Renaissance
The dawning of a new day
Where every man is a king and every woman a queen

This is the Renaissance
What a renaissance
This is the Renaissance

This is the Renaissance
What a renaissance
This is the Renaissance

We can see the moon
We can see the stars
We can see the future and
The freeways and electric cars
And they might think we're quaint
We don't really care
We've got Michelangelo and they graffiti everywhere

'Cause, this is the Renaissance
Came upon us all at once
Oh, what a renaissance
This is the Renaissance
Renaissance or Renàissance
It's still a renaissance

Bullet Train

It's the bullet train, bullet train, bullet train, yeah
It's a miracle, a miracle, a miracle, yeah
It's the bullet train, bullet train, bullet train, yeah
It's immaculate, immaculate, immaculate, yeah

It's improbable, improbable, improbable, yeah
It's the bullet train, bullet train, bullet train, yeah
It's impeccable, impeccable, impeccable, yeah
It's the bullet train, bullet train, bullet train, yeah

It's the bullet train, faster and faster, oh yeah
It's the bullet train, faster and faster, oh yeah
It's the bullet train, faster and faster, oh yeah
It's the bullet train, faster and faster, oh yeah

Can't we work this out between us, can't we
work it all out
Can't we work this out, work this out, work it all out
I should learn from those around us to be
more roundabout
Can't we come to some solution, can't we
work it all out

And to the right, Fuji, Mt. Fuji, oh wow
Yes, to the right, the rarest sight, Mt. Fuji, oh wow
We can count ourselves lucky, oh so lucky, oh wow
It's the rarest sight, Fuji, not hidden by clouds

If you're gonna cry, better wait, do it at home
It you're gonna cry, gonna cry, do it at home
On the bullet train, nobody, nobody cries
No one's ever cried, never, on the bullet train, no

It's the bullet train, bullet train, bullet train, yeah
It's a miracle, a miracle, a miracle, yeah
It's the bullet train, bullet train, bullet train, yeah
It's immaculate, immaculate, immaculate, yeah

It's improbable, improbable, improbable, yeah
It's the bullet train, bullet train, bullet train, yeah
It's impeccable, impeccable, impeccable, yeah
It's the bullet train, bullet train, bullet train, yeah

It's a testament, a testament to science and art
It's a testament, a testament to who that we are
It's a monument, a monument to science and art
It's a monument, a monument to who that we are

It's proficiency, proficiency, proficiency, yeah
It's efficiency, efficiency, efficiency, yeah
How the fabric and the finish and the glass intersect

It's the bullet train, bullet train,
so what's next?

Perfume

Genevieve wears Dior
Margaret wears Tresor
Mary Jo wears Lauren
But you don't wear no perfume

Deborah wears Clinique
Marianne wears Mystique
Judith wears Shalimar
But you don't wear no perfume

That's why I want to spend my life with you
That's why I want to spend my life with you
That's why I want to spend my life with you

Anna wears CK One
Jeanie wears Opium
Trisha wears No. 5
But you don't wear no perfume

Susan wears St. Laurent
Janie wears L'Air du Temps
Kristin wears Davidoff
But you don't wear no perfume

That's why I want to spend my life with you
That's why I want to spend my life with you
That's why I want to spend my life with you

The olfactory sense is the sense that most strongly
evokes memories of the past
Well, screw the past

That's why I want to spend my life with you
That's why I want to spend my life with you
That's why I want to spend my life with you

Genevieve wears Hermès
Annabelle wears Arpège
Betty Lee wears Guerlain
But you don't wear no perfume

Katie wears Giorgio
Lily wears Moschino
Jenna wears Kenneth Cole
But you don't wear no perfume

That's why I want to spend my life with you
That's why I want to spend my life with you
That's why I want to spend my life with you

Carol wears Cacharel
Lana wears Tommy Girl
Cynthia wears J'Adore
But you don't wear no perfume

Jennifer wears Celine
Laura wears Armani
Deborah wears Polo Sport
But you don't wear no perfume

Gina wears Vera Wang
Sheila wears Helmut Lang
Diana wears Oxygene
But you don't wear no perfume

Jody wears Gaultier
Peggy wears Jean Patou
Stella wears Lagerfeld
But you don't wear no perfume

That's why I want to spend my life with you
That's why I want to spend my life with you
That's why I want to spend my life with you

That's why, that's why
That's why, that's why
That's why, that's why
That's why, that's why

How Do I Get To Carnegie Hall?

How do I get to Carnegie Hall?
How do I get to Carnegie Hall?
How do I get to Carnegie Hall?

Practice, man, practice
Practice, man, practice
Practice, man, practice
Practice, man, practice

How do I get to Carnegie Hall?
Practice, man, practice
How do I get to Carnegie Hall?
Practice, man, practice
To get yourself to Carnegie Hall
Practice, man, practice
How do I get to Carnegie Hall?
Carnegie Hall, Carnegie Hall

Technical facility
Old-word sensibility
All of this I did for you
Still there is no sign of you

I practiced, I practiced
Carnegie Hall was beckoning
I practiced, I practiced
Carnegie Hall was beckoning
I was ready, I was ready
Carnegie Hall was beckoning

Still there is no sign of you
Still there is no sign of you

Steinway, Steinway, Steinway, Steinway

How do I get to Carnegie Hall?
Practice, man, practice
How do I get to Carnegie Hall?
Practice, man, practice
To get yourself to Carnegie Hall
Practice, man, practice
How do I get to Carnegie Hall?
Carnegie Hall, Carnegie Hall

Practice on the Steinway
Practice on the Steinway
Practice on the Steinway

Practice, practice

They loved it, they showed it
The audience was deafening
I was ready, I was ready
The critics all said, "riveting"
On the Steinway, on the Steinway
I guess it doesn't mean a thing

Still there is no sign of you
Still there is no sign of you

How do I get to Carnegie Hall?
Practice, man, practice
How do I get to Carnegie Hall?
Practice, man, practice
How do I get to Carnegie Hall?
Practice, man, practice

I practiced, I practiced

Bravo, bravo, bravo, bravo

How do I get to Carnegie Hall?
Practice, man, practice
How do I get to Carnegie Hall?
Practice, man, practice
How do I get to Carnegie Hall?
It don't mean a thing

Still there is no sign of you
Still there is no sign of you

Achoo

Who knows what the winds gonna bring
    when the invalids sing
"La la's" with a powerful string that'll stop
 any opera or any Bing
 Sing, spread the news across the land
 All winners will be also-rans
 Achoo – one size fits everyone
 Achoo – one breath, the deed has been done

 Grey hair and a dash and a flair give your
 doctor an air
 I'm hurt, but the choice that you made
 is an obvious one
 For a girl who needs care
 I do hope that he makes you well
 Say, is there any cure for Hell,
 Achoo – one size fits everyone
 Achoo – one breath, the deed has been done

 Sing, Île-de-France and everywhere
 You can't ignore that sort of air
 Achoo – one size fits everyone
 Achoo – one breath, the deed has been done

 So, open wide, open wide and say, open wide
 and say goodbye, you'll be OK

 Achoo – he's gonna whisk you away
 Achoo – he's gonna make you OK

Whippings And Apologies

Whippings and apologies
Over and over they did it to her when she disagreed
Whippings and apologies
Over and over and over and over
You know it's not right
For she has holy water running through her veins
And now it's me that she hates, it's me that she hates

Whippings + apologies
Over + over they did it to her when
    she disagreed

Whippings + Apologies
Over + over + over + over
and you know that that's not
    right
Cause she has holy water running
    thru her veins
And now it's me that she hates
me that she hate

Without Using Hands

The canopy over the main doorway
of the Ritz Hotel
Had served as a very large umbrella
when the May rains fell
Still the men of Paris glistened
and their ladies did as well
As long as their powder was dry
there'd be some heterosexual thrills
With or without the protection
of the Paris Ritz Hotel

And every single Parisian will love tonight
without using hands

And these are the slides that Mary took
when we were overseas
Oh, look at the funny little Frenchmen
with some French company
There's the Ritz Hotel where me
and Mary stayed a couple of days
Jerry, let go of your sister, what is wrong
with you today
Sit over there with your mother and let's sing
La Marseillaise

The only way children are punished,
unlike old times is without using hands

Oh, what a lovely city, city, city, city

Oh, what a lovely city, city, city, city
Oh, what a lovely city, city, city, city
Oh, what a lovely city, city, city, city
Oh, are you willing to go
Oh, are you willing to go
How about letting me know, without using hands

When the explosion rocked the lobby
of the Ritz Hotel
Nobody moved for fear of learning
that they weren't all that well
Is there is anybody missing,
answer only if you're well
Everyone cheered the good fortune,
for indeed it turned out well
Only the manager suffered,
but at least his face looks swell

The manager is going to live his entire life
without using hands

Without using hands

Rock, Rock, Rock

Soft passages (they get you into trouble)
They imply a lack of passion and commitment

Soft passages (they get you into trouble)
They imply a lack of feeling and of fervor

They get you into trouble
They get you into trouble
They imply a certain air of indecision

Soft passages (they get you into trouble)
And since you put a gun to my head…

I promise that I'll
Rock, rock, rock
Don't leave me, don't leave me, don't leave me, don't leave me
I will rock, rock, rock
Like a mother, like a mother, like a mother, like a mother

Soft passages can get you into trouble
They imply a lack of passion and commitment
Soft passages can get you into trouble
(They get you into trouble)
They get you into trouble

I promise that I'll
Rock, rock, rock
Don't leave me, don't leave me, don't leave me, don't leave me
I will rock, rock, rock
Like a mother, like a mother, like a mother, like a mother

A lack of passion
A lack of commitment
A lack of feeling
A lack of fervor
A lack of decisiveness
And since you put a gun to my head...

I promise that I'll
Rock, rock, rock
Don't leave me, don't leave me, don't leave me, don't leave me
I will rock, rock, rock
Like a mother, like a mother, like a mother, like a mother

Soft passages (they get you into trouble)
They imply a certain poor respectability
A certain measure of weakness (they get you into trouble)
A certain level of maturity

I promise that I'll
Rock, rock, rock
Don't leave me, don't leave me, don't leave me, don't leave me
I will rock, rock, rock
Like a mother, like a mother, like a mother, like a mother

Don't leave me, don't leave me, don't leave me, don't leave me
Like a mother, like a mother, like a mother, like a mother
Don't leave me, don't leave me, don't leave me, don't leave me
Like a mother, like a mother, like a mother, like a mother

A lack of passion
A lack of commitment
A lack of feeling
A lack of fervor
A lack of decisiveness
And since you put a gun to my head...

I promise that I'll
Rock, rock, rock
Don't leave me, don't leave me, don't leave me, don't leave me
I will rock, rock, rock
Like a mother, like a mother, like a mother, like a mother

And since you put, and since you put, and since you put, and since
you put, and since you put a gun to my head...

I promise that I'll
Rock, rock, rock
Don't leave me, don't leave me, don't leave me, don't leave me (rock,
rock, rock)
I will rock, rock, rock
Like a mother, like a mother, like a mother, like a mother (rock,
rock, rock)

I promise that I'll
Rock, rock, rock
Don't leave me, don't leave me, don't leave me, don't leave me (rock,
rock, rock)
I will rock, rock, rock
Rock, rock, rock

I Bought The Mississippi River

I bought the Mississippi River
Of course that don't include the towns
Or the people
Around the Mississippi
Well, to cinch the deal the man threw
In a boat with crew
And then I knew I'd better grab that river fast
It wouldn't last
They never do, they never do
It wouldn't last, last, last

So now I own the Mississippi
I couldn't decide if I should leave it there
Or lug it out West with me
Well, the best was to think about
Not to make a move I might regret
Cause then I'd have to have the
Mississippi sent back East, complete
With boat and crew
That wouldn't do, do, do

It's mine, all mine
(You know, it's yours, all yours)
It's mine, all mine
(You know, it's yours, all yours)

Do rivers ever need companions
Should I enquire if the Seine is
Available, yeah, I would rather have
A classy little Frenchy than a Nile or a Tiba, oh
Now wait a minute, how about the
Amazon, now that could be real fun
For Mississippi, for Mississippi, for

Mississippi, My Mississippi
(It's yours, all yours)

Those Mysteries

Why is there time
Why is there space
Why are there dogs and cats
And trees and the human race
And why am I here and not over there
Oh why, oh why oh why, oh why
And why are there nuns
And why do they pray
And where do we go when we pass away
And why, when I ask my Dad does he say
Go ask your Mom or just go away
And O.K., I'll go away, but they won't go away

Those mysteries
Tomorrow I'll find out all I should know
Those mysteries
I don't even know what I don't even know
Those mysteries
They're hanging around
And around and around and around

Why is there you
Why is there me
Why does my Mother kiss my Father occasionally
And why am I sore whenever I'm hit
Oh why, oh why oh why, oh why
And why is there France
And why is there Spain
And why am I here and why is there rain
And why, when I ask my Dad does he say

Go ask your Mom or just go away
And O.K., I'll go away, but they won't go away

Those mysteries
Tomorrow I'll find out all I should know
Those mysteries
I don't even know what I don't even know
Those mysteries
They're hanging around
And around and around and around

Why is there time
Why is there space

Girl From Germany

How I wished that my folks were gracious hosts
and not dismayed
But wit and wisdom take a backseat,
girl, when you're that afraid
Oh no, bring her home and the folks look ill
My word, they can't forget, they never will

They can hear the storm troops on our lawn
when I show her in
And the Führer is alive and well in our paneled den
Oh no, bring her home and the folks look ill
My word, they can't forget that war, what a war

My word, she's from Germany
Well, it's the same old country but the people have changed
My word... Germany
With its splendid castles and its fine cuisine

Well, the car I drive is parked outside, it's German-made
They resent that less than the people who are German-made
Oh no, bring her home and the folks look ill
My word, they can't forget that war, what a war, some war

My word... Germany
Well, it's the same old country but the people have changed
My word... Germany
With its splendid castles and its fine cuisine

How I wished my folks were gracious hosts & not dismayed
But wit & wisdom take a back seat when you're that afraid
[Oh no, bring her home & the folks look ill]
[Oh no, they can't forget, they never will]

They can hear the storm troops on our lawn when I show her in
And the fuehrer is alive & well in our paneled den living room
[Oh no, bring her home & the folks look ill]
[Oh no, they can't forget that war, what a war!]

{ Oh no, she's from Germany, it's that same old country but the people have changed
{ Oh no, she's from Germany, with its splendid castles & fine cuisine

The car I drive is parked outside, it's German made
They resent that less than people who are German made
{ Oh no, bring her home & the folks look ill
{ Oh no, they can't forget that war, that war

{ Oh no, she's from Germany, it's that same old country, but the people have changed
{ Oh no, she's from Germany, with it's splendid castles & fine cuisine

How I wished my folks were gracious hosts & not dismayed
Wit & wisdom take a back seat when you're that afraid
[Oh no, bring her home & the folks look ill
[Oh no, they can't forget that war, what a war!

{ Oh no, she's from Germany, it's the same old country, but the people have changed
{ Oh no, she's from Germany, land of and German beer

Girl From Germany

Its lovely German women, its wonderful rivers that do flow
from her hills

My word, she's from Germany
Well, it's the same old country but the people have changed
My word, she's from Germany
With its splendid castles and its fine cuisine

My word, she's from Germany
Well, it's the same old country but the people have changed
My word, she's from Germany
With its splendid castles and its fine cuisine

My word, she's from Germany
Well, it's the same old country but the people have changed
My word, she's from Germany
With its splendid castles, its fine cuisine, its lovely German
women and you and me!

Popularity

I like you and you like me a lot
And we do those things that can make us feel hot
Then we join some friends, all of them are all right
And we talk a while, then we climb in our cars

What a night, we all drive into town
Where we'll park our cars, and meet the rest of our friends
At a place that's called, I forget what it's called
But it's really great, and all our friends will be there

Popularity
Popularity

I like you and you like me a lot
And it's nice to be all alone with you too
But it's also nice being out with our friends
'Cause they're all alright, maybe that's why we're friends

Popularity
Popularity

I feel great, but it's getting real late
So I'll drive you home and you'll slide up real close
I'm so glad we met, and I like you so much
And I'm also glad that I got all those friends

Popularity
Popularity

Sisters

There's a round-up at the love corral
and the air is full of dust
And I think it's going pretty well
but I'm trying to adjust
As we walk along the boulevard
with a hand in hand in hand
And who cares if people stare at us
'cause they'll never understand

Sisters
Where is the jealousy, is it there
Sisters
Is this a felony anywhere
Who cares
I see a double moon in the sky
Sisters
An oversupply

Do I have to be a diplomat
when I hear you fuss and fight
Do I have to be an acrobat
as I try to set it right
There's a double moon up in the sky
and it's shining down on me
And I know that I'm a lucky guy
that's my biography

Sisters
Where is the jealousy, is it there
Sisters
Is this a felony anywhere
Who cares
I see a double moon in the sky

Sisters
An oversupply

My arms are full
My lips are sore
By morning we could face the light

And I know if I lose one of you
I would feel a little down
Well, it wouldn't be disastrous
I would still have you around

Sisters
Where is the jealousy, is it there
Sisters
Is this a felony anywhere
Who cares
I see a double moon in the sky
Sisters
An oversupply

Aeroflot

I don't know about you, but I'm sitting pretty
We're flying Aeroflot, we're flying Aeroflot
Vodka on ice, and a hostess who's witty
We're flying Aeroflot, we're flying Aeroflot

Buckle up, buckle up, buckle up, daddy-o
Stow your bags overhead or it ain't a go
Buckle up, buckle up, buckle up, daddy-o
You never know, you never know, do you

We're flying Aeroflot, we're flying Aeroflot, we're
flying Aeroflot
We've got reservations

I don't know about you, but I love adventure
We're flying Aeroflot, we're flying Aeroflot
On Aeroflot, every flight's an adventure
We're flying Aeroflot, we're flying Aeroflot

Stretch on out, daddy-o, we're talking space
Every pilot is an honored MiG Ace
Leningrad, St. Petersburg, in either case
You never know, you never you, do you

We're flying Aeroflot, we're flying Aeroflot, we're
flying Aeroflot
We've got reservations

Way back in coach they're singing 'Viva Vacation'
We're flying Aeroflot, we're flying Aeroflot

Up here in business is the United Nations
We're flying Aeroflot, we're flying Aeroflot

Blinis on your plate and Eisenstein on screen
Richard Branson must be turning red or green
Stewardesses look like high school beauty queens
They never say "nyet," service supreme, supreme

We're flying Aeroflot, we're flying Aeroflot, we're
flying Aeroflot
We've got reservations

"Thank you for flying Aeroflot"

Lost And Found

Lost and found, a wallet from a man,
careless man, careless man
Too bad, too bad, too bad, too bad

Lost and found, a wallet from a man,
careless man, careless man
And all the streets are paved tonight,
and we won't be their slaves tonight
And I ain't gonna feel bad at all, feel bad at all

Lost and found, a wallet from a man,
careless man, careless man
Too bad, too bad, too bad, too bad
Lost and found, a wallet from a man,
careless man, careless man

He's Robin Hood by accident
I need it more than he does and
I surely will not feel bad at all, feel bad at all,
feel bad at all, feel bad at all

Lost and found, a wallet from a man,
careless man, careless man
Oh, is there anybody out there by the name of
Mister Jones?
No? No? Well, I tried

Lost and found, lost and found,
lost and found, lost and found

Lost and found, a wallet from a man,
careless man, careless man
Too bad, too bad, too bad, too bad
Lost and found, a wallet from a man,
careless man, careless man

We sailed across the Barbary Sea
With Nina, Pinta, and Marie
And none of us will feel bad at all, feel bad at all,
feel bad at all, feel bad at all

Yes, all the streets are paved tonight, and we won't
be their slaves tonight
And I ain't gonna feel bad at all, feel bad at all
Lost and found, lost and found, lost and found,
lost and found

Change

The rain is falling down
I feel like a dog that's been kicked out into the street
I know that dogs can't drive cars
But that's about the only difference between us now

But wait, there's a rainbow over the freeway
And I think I feel the morning sun
Another song is number one
Golden days have just begun

Change. Every dog is gonna have his day
Change. Every loser's gonna have his way
Change. I don't care what other people say

Well, you can't argue all day long about whether
love really exists or not
It's a complete waste of time
Like arguing about whether Santa Claus really
exists or not
I got better things to do with my time

I got places that I've gotta be
And people that I've gotta see
Mountains that I have to ski
Golden days ahead of me

Change. Every dog is gonna have his day
Change. Every loser's gonna have his way
Change. I don't care what other people say
Change. I know everything will be OK

Paradise was here, paradise is gone
Greece and Rome were here,
Greece and Rome are gone
The Wild West was here, the Wild West is gone
Vaudeville was here, Vaudeville is gone

Change. Every dog is gonna have his day
Change. I don't care what other people say

You know I've been thinkin' we'll get back
together again someday
Your hair will be some weird color by then
Maybe we'll just start off again as friends
I wonder when

Change. Every dog is gonna have his day
Change. Every loser's gonna have his way
Change. I don't care what other people say
Change. I know everything will be OK
Change. Every dog is gonna have his day
Change. Every loser's gonna have his way
Change. I don't care what other people say
Change. Just ignore them and they'll go away

The Rhythm Thief

I am the rhythm thief
Say goodbye to the beat
I am the rhythm thief
Auf wiedersehen to the beat

Oh no, where did the groove go, where did the groove
go, where did the groove go?
Lights out, Ibiza
Where did the groove go, where did the groove go,
where did the groove go?

You'll never get it back, you'll never get it back,
The rhythm thief has got it and you'll never get it back
You'll never get it back, you'll never get it back,
The rhythm thief has got it and you'll never get it back
You'll never get it back, you'll never get it back,
The rhythm thief has got it and you'll never get it back

Lights out, Ibiza
I am the rhythm thief
Goodbye, goodbye, goodbye

Gratuitous Sax

You need another relative, you need it right away
What should I do, what should I do?
Another entertainment so that they won't go away
I thought of you and how you blew 'til you were blue
Throw in some
Gratuitous sax

What Are All These Bands So Angry About?

Hey everybody, what do you know
What are all these bands so angry about?

Hey everybody, what do you say
Someone's stolen our spotlight, Ray
Hey everybody, what do you say
What are all these bands so angry about?

Hey everybody, what do you know
Something's stolen our thunder, Joe
Hey everybody, what do you know
What are all these bands so angry about?

Hey everybody, what can we do?
Crank it up just a notch or two?
Hey, everybody, what can we do?
What are all these bands so angry about?

Hey everybody, they called our bluff
Our profane ain't profane enough
Hey everybody, they called our bluff
What are all these bands so angry about?

Hey everybody, what do you say
Someone's bounced us from center stage

Some might have done it, but not today
Beethoven, Coltrane, or Lady Day
Some might have done it, but not today
What with all these things besieging us now

Some might have done it, broken on through
Wagner, Tatum, or Howlin' Wolf
Some might have done what we'll never do
What are all these bands so angry about?

Hey everybody, what do you know
Something's stolen our thunder, Joe
Hey everybody, what do you know
What are all these bands so angry about?

The Very Next Fight

The very next fight
I have over you
Will end up the same
It's always the same

The very next fight
From out of the blue (it's always the same)
Will end up the same
It's always the same (it's always the same)

Some idiot staring at your legs, I know
You quietly tell me I should let it go
But how can I let it go
When I can't control myself
How can I let it go
When I cannot help myself

It's always the same (it's always the same)

The very next fight
I have over you
Will end up the same
It's always the same

The very next fight
From out of the blue (it's always the same)
Will end up the same
It's always the same (it's always the same)

Blood on the floor of some posh restaurant
Deep down I'm sure this is what you want
And what you want, is what I want.

What you want, is what I want.
It's always the same (it's always the same)
Open displays of affection
It's always the same (it's always the same)

The very next fight
From out of the blue (it's always the same)
Will end up the same
It's always the same (it's always the same)

Some idiot staring at your legs, I know
You quietly tell me I should let it go
But how can I let it go
When I can't control myself
How can I let it go
When I cannot help myself

It's always the same (it's always the same)

The very next fight
I have over you
Will end up the same
It's always the same

The very next fight (it's always the same)
From out of the blue (it's always the same)
Will end up the same (it's always the same)
It's always the same (it's always the same)

Open displays of affection

Instant Weight Loss

Don't play that riff
Don't play that riff
Don't play that riff
That takes me back
Instant weight loss

There was this girl
Black hair, so what
She called me Fats
But in one night
Instant weight loss

One night, one steamy night
I'd lose a kilo each hour
In ten nights, ten steamy nights
And figure, a kilo an hour
Instant weight loss

Then came this guy
Some foreign name
Had chubby hands
Wore lots of chains
Instant weight loss

That's it
What's done is done
Erase the past if you can
With ice cream, with coconut pie
In less than a week I am done
Instant weight loss

Don't play that riff
She sang that riff
All through the night
It's coming back
I've gained an ounce
I've gained a pound
Another pound
I've gained a ton

So last July
This girl pulls up
Blonde hair, so what
She says, "Hey Fats"
Instant weight loss

My Other Voice

You're so independent but that's gonna
   change real soon
With my other voice I can destroy this room
I'll wrap my voice around you
and I'll drag you everywhere
My other voice

You think you're romantic,
well I'll whisper in your ear
I'll be all you'll hear for years and years and years
You may be deaf to everything,
you won't be deaf to me
My other voice

National Crime Awareness Week

On and on, the world keeps spinning
On and on, I keep on winning

This is a case of passion over reason
This is a case when your shoes don't need a shine
Gimme some space, man, to practice my profession
I've got the ace, man, and what is yours is mine
In theory, yes, I abhor the violence
In practice, well, sometimes they freak

You honor me
I feel unique
It's National Crime Awareness Week

I'll put it to you this way, I love to take chances
I'll put it to you this way, I'm a happy, happy guy
I'll put it to you this way, I love the little headlines
"Unknown Caucasian Strikes One More Time"

So, don't say a word, just hand me the Timex
I've got places to go and people to meet

You honor me
I feel unique
It's National Crime Awareness Week

Every time you shower, are you waiting for the music
The curtain drawing back, the water turning red
Don't blame that on me, I ain't no Tony Perkins
I'm saner than you are, I know that for a fact

On and on, the world keeps spinning
On and on, I keep on winning

Maybe next year you'll bring my streak
During National Crime Awareness Week
But as for now I've got mystique
During National Crime Awareness Week

Hey, you honor me
I feel unique
It's National Crime Awareness Week

Hear No Evil, See No Evil, Speak No Evil

I'm the wife of Clinton
I don't have a problem with all of this
They come and go, of course I know, I know everything
You don't know my thinking,
who I dream of or the gifts that I bring
One thing is clear, the atmosphere is thin and it's cold

Hear no evil (Monkey 1 says you shouldn't hear it)
See no evil (Monkey 2 says you shouldn't see it)
Speak no evil (Monkey 3 says you shouldn't speak it)

I am Madame Mao
Following the Tao to the extreme
I know the score, all this and more, they're still in their teens
You don't know my thinking,
who I dream of, or the gifts that I bring
One thing is true, I won't leave clues, to where I have been

Hear no evil (Monkey 1 says you shouldn't hear it)
See no evil (Monkey 2 says you shouldn't see it)
Speak no evil (Monkey 3 says you shouldn't speak it)

We on the Potomac love good times
We on the Yangtze love good times
We on the Nile love good times
Can't get enough of good times
More than enough love to go 'round
More than enough power to go 'round
More than enough ids to be found
More than enough bids to go down

Hear no evil (Monkey 1 says you shouldn't hear it)
See no evil (Monkey 2 says you shouldn't see it)
Speak no evil (Monkey 3 says you shouldn't speak it)

I am Cleopatra, Caesar's gone forever, now I am yours
Marc Antony, you're biting off more than you can chew

Monkey 1 says you shouldn't hear it
Monkey 2 says you shouldn't see it
Monkey 3 says you shouldn't speak it

Hear no evil
See no evil
Speak no evil

Photoshop

Stars made you look younger
Sadness is erased
Baldness or aloofness
Gone without a trace
Signs, you know the way to make men men
To make "Miss Everyday" a 10
To think you used to be my friend

Photoshop me out of your life

There you see a billboard
Faces super smooth
There an illustration
Whiteness, every tooth
Signs, you've worked your magic once again
It's always better in the end
To think you used to be my friend

Photoshop me out of your life

Every blemish is gone in a flash
Lines that are crooked and colors that clash
Every blemish is gone in a flash
Lines that are crooked and colors that clash

Photoshop me out of your life

You know what you're doing
Look at the acclaim
Grant me one more favor
Alter the terrain
Make it look as though I were in Hell
Or something near enough to Hell
Or something near enough to Hell
Give it a caption of "Farewell"

Photoshop me out of your life

Le guide me montre et explique
"Celui ci est le changement"
Les touristes s'en donnent à coeur joie
Ils touchent mon marbre froid
Mais mes yeux sont fixer sur la porte

Je sais pourtant que j'dois rester
Parmis tous ces héros tués
Protégeant leur liberté de vivre dans des musées
Mais mes yeux sont fixer sur la porte

Essayez donc de m'enlever
Je voudrais voir si vous oser

Quelqu'un a entendu ma supplique
Depuis quelques heures, je vole
Mais à l'aurore elle me quitteras
Et les murs se refermeront sur moi
Il ne restera plus que le marbre froid

The tourist guide explains my aims
"This one's a monument to change."
The tourists do marvel, they touch my cold marble
But my eyes are fixed upon the door

Let's see you lift me
I dare you to try
Let's see you lift me
I dare you to try
Let's see you raise me
I dare you to try
Let's see you lift me
I dare you to try
Let's see you lift me
I dare you to try

Pineapple

Tropical air helps us harvest all year
  And serves to promote the vitamin C content
In turn yielding greater demand

Pineapple
Got to send a case to the city jail
The warden likes it because it won't conceal
Any sort of handmade weapons
That are baked right into their buns
And the taste is delectable

But won't the prisoners hit the table and shout
Pineapple, pineapple, pineapple fulfills every need
Pineapple (shares are gonna divide)
Pineapple (if in us you confide)

Got a contract for all of the schools
They will use it for all of their meals
Sure, the kids will throw it real far
'Cause it ain't a milk chocolate bar
But you know it don't stain so bad

But won't they fling it at a friend and then shout
Pineapple (tastes too healthy to me)
Pineapple (it's filled with vitamin C)
Pineapple fulfills every need
Pineapple (to all the ships at sea)
Pineapple (for the English at tea)
Pineapple (to the Siamese twins)
Pineapple (to heal those who have sinned)

Ship some to the Alpine skiing team
The coach won't have to worry 'bout the calories
Sure it ain't strudel (they're nice)
But it helps your balance on ice
Puts you back on the winning trail

But don't the players moan and groan and then shout:
Pineapple (we get it every old night)
Pineapple (but we're winning all right)
Pineapple fulfills every need
Pineapple (shares are gonna divide)
Pineapple (if in us you confide)
Pineapple fulfills every need
Pineapple (upward trends are foreseen)
Pineapple (so invest in Big P)
Pineapple fulfills every need
Pineapple (and the tins can be used)
Pineapple (for anything that you choose)
Pineapple, pineapple

We'll jet you there, breathe the Hawaiian air
Where hula is life, and luaus are for the wife
So visit our factory soon

Nothing To Do

I want you
I want you bad
I need you
I need you
I do, I really do

Better drop the requirement
that everything be great
Nothing to do, nothing to do
Nothing to do, nothing to do

I come home (nothing to do)
I throw my coat down (nothing to do)
I spin round (nothing to do)
I plop down (nothing to do)
Gimme a break, a little break

Better drop the requirement
that everything be great
Nothing to do, nothing to do
Nothing to do, nothing to do

Well, if I had a million thumbs
I'd twiddle, twiddle
But I just have two

Nothing to do, nothing to do

Nothing to do, nothing to do

I see you (nothing to do)
I don't want much (nothing to do)
Just something (nothing to do)
A little something
To do, to do

Better drop the requirement
that everything be great
Nothing to do, nothing to do
Nothing to do, nothing to do

The Wedding Of Jacqueline Kennedy To Russell Mael

Mr. Jones is unavailable at the moment
However, if you wish to leave a message,
please do so after the tone.

Do you Jacqueline Kennedy, take Russell Mael
To be your lawful wedded husband, in sickness and in health
For richer or for poorer, for better or for worse
Till death do you part?

"I do."

And do you Russell Mael, take Jacqueline Kennedy
To be your lawful wedded wife, in sickness and in health
For richer or for poorer, for better or for worse
Till death do you part?

"I do."

Then I now pronounce you man and wife

Looks Aren't Everything

Looks aren't everything

I bought a car, it's yellow
I drove around a lot
I caught a fish and fried it
I ate it on the spot – hot

And that's my year in review
With you things could be different

Looks aren't everything
Looks aren't everything
Looks aren't everything

By Jove, I think I've got it
By Jove, it's come at last
By Jove, there's wrinkles on it
By Jove, it's come at last

For the one who has made us all
Can't be seen even if you're tall
Looks aren't everything

Sleep sound and dream, you've earned it
A most impressive day
Deeds and props rewarded
It's almost Saturday – say!

I like you more when the view and you are
less than perfect

Looks aren't everything
Looks aren't everything
Looks aren't everything

Wake up the dawn's upon us
No don't go run and hide
I've got some jokes to tell you
And God is on your side

For the one who has made us all
Can't be seen even if you're tall

Looks aren't everything

We're moving to the city
Where we'll get softer hands
And nature's non-existent
But there they understand that

Looks aren't everything

By Jove, I think we've got it
By Jove, it's come at last
By Jove, there's wrinkles on it
By Jove, it's come at last

For the one who has made us all
Can't be seen even by the tall
For the one who has made us all
Can't be seen even if you're tall

Looks aren't everything

Over The Summer

Over the summer, over the summer, over the summer

You've got to trust in summer
Miracles can happen if you do
'Cause all that heat speeds change in everything
Maybe even you

If you're a summertime believer
If you're a summertime believer
July, you were the plainest of Janes
Through August, you got rearranged
September, you're not just a brain
Over the summer, over the summer, over the summer

I tried to find myself this summertime
I found you instead
And please forgive me Karen, but in June
You were kind of dead

But, then we had that three-day hot spell
You really turned into a bombshell
July, you were the plainest of Janes
Through August, you got rearranged
September, you're not just a brain
Over the summer, over the summer, over the summer

Over the summer, you're under the summer sun
Over the summer, you're under the summer sun
Over the summer, you're under the summer sun
Lying there, lying there, lying there, getting hot

You know the records that I got in June
Don't sound good no more
And all the clothes I bought in June
Are now rotting in my drawers

But you're a different girl, much better
A little redder, but much better
Was it just the heat of the sun
Was it that you had lots of fun
I wish that the summer weren't done
Over the summer, over the summer, over the summer

The Number One Song In Heaven

This is the number one song in heaven
Written, of course, by the mightiest hand
All of the angels are sheep in the fold of their master
They always follow the Master and his plan

This is the number one song in heaven
Why are you hearing it now, you ask
Maybe you're closer to here than you imagine
Maybe you're closer to here than you care to be

It's number one, all over heaven
It's number one, all over heaven
It's number one, all over heaven
The number one song all over heaven

If you should die before you wake
If you should die while crossing the street
The song that you'll hear, I guarantee

It's number one, all over heaven
It's number one, all over heaven
It's number one, all over heaven
The number one song all over heaven

The one that's the rage up here in the clouds
Loud as a crowd or soft as a doubt

Lyrically weak, but the music's the thing

Gabriel plays it, God, how he plays it
Gabriel plays it, God, how he plays it
Gabriel plays it, God, how he plays it
Gabriel plays it, let's hear him play it

The song filters down, down through the clouds
It reaches the Earth and winds all around
And then it breaks up in millions of ways

It goes la, la, la....

In cars it becomes a hit
And in your homes it becomes advertisements
And in the streets it becomes children singing

Batteries Not Included

I bought it home and I opened it up
And a smile came to my face for the first time in a while
Yes, a smile came to my face for the first time in a while
I turned it on
But nothing happened when I did
Nothing happened at all
I kicked it down the stairs
I threw it at the wall

"Hey kid, batteries not included"

Looks, Looks, Looks

Looks, looks, looks
You had sense, you had style, you had cash galore
Looks, looks, looks
You employed her and dressed her in formal fashion
Still you bore her because you ain't got a
Nose that's straight, a set of perfect teeth
You got a built-in seat, that makes you look effete
You know that looks, looks, looks, are why you
rely on books

Looks, looks, looks
From the eye to the brain's just an inch or two
Looks, looks, looks
From the eye to the heart's only slightly farther
the smart grow smarter, but still can't complete
And they know deep down that they are scarred for life
And that a face can launch a thousand hips
It's gonna be all right
If it ain't, don't blame me, it's your looks

At night she masquerades her passion covered
by a veil of calm
Say, put on your shoes
Say, put on your shoes
No use, one look at her and anyone can tell
that she's on fire

Spot her error, spot her error, spot her error
Well, now she's all over you

LLL
Though the good may die young they die looking good
LLL
And the angels may fall for you just because of
LLL

★

LLL
No it's not very hard to make history
LLL
Just some cavalry and a good uniform that
fits in places where everyone tends to
Look and marvel at the way you lead them out
Look and marvel at the way you win because of
Looks, looks, looks
As long as you're long on looks

★

LLL
From the eye to the brains just an inch or two
LLL
From the eye to the hearts only slightly farther
The smart grow smarter but still can't compete
And they know down in their hearts
they're scared for life
And that a face can
Launch a thousand   Looks, look, look
trips
It alright + it ain't
don't blame me
it's your looks

Looks, Looks, Looks

til you are blue in the face

slay but

er, looks
y close at hand it's the only thing

seas ~~en~~ in the sand any place is laced with those
~~I only thing that's quite life~~ long   who have it ~~re~~
~~eatly matters~~   and those ~~attempt~~ ~~already made to~~
~~help~~ ~~haven't~~ skill ine   to ~~try~~ ~~hide the their lack of it~~
                                             or ~~learn~~ a skill ~~is back~~ buttons
                                             or always, ~~sit~~ is back
                                             looks, looks, looks
                                             ~~teach me learn to cook~~
                                             ~~keep~~ you
                                             make them put down their books ~~for 7~~

I know lots of those facts cause I'm shoton looks ~~lots T~~
Look long on details
And longer agan

~~I had sense~~
~~galore~~

~~ber and~~
~~formal fashion~~
~~her~~ before her
~~can't get a~~

<u>Mid</u>
At night she masquerades, her passion covered by a veil of calm
say, put on your shoos,
say, put on your shoes

No use, one look at her and anyone can tell that she's on fire
Spot her error
Spot her error
Spot her error
Now ~~@~~ she's all over ~~me~~ you

on ~~books~~

Looks, looks, looks
No, it's not very hard to make history
Looks, looks, looks
Just some cavalry and a good uniform that fits in places
Where everyone tends to look and marvel
At the way you lead them on and
Look and marvel at the way you win because of
Looks, looks, looks
As long as you're long on looks

Spot her error, spot her error, spot he error
Well, now she's all over you

Looks, looks, looks
Far away, close at hand, it's the only thing
Looks, looks, looks
On the seas in the sand, any place is laced with
those who have it
And those who can only look

I Can't Believe
That You Would Fall
For All The Crap
In This Song

I want you
And only you and only you, my love
I need you
And only you and only you, my love

I can't believe that you would fall for all the crap in this song
I can't believe that you would fall for all the crap in this song

Forever you, forever you, my love
And only you, and only you, my love
Forever you, forever you, my love
And only you, and only you, my love

I want you
And only you and only you, my love
I need you
And only you and only you, my love

I can't believe that you would fall for all the crap in this song
I can't believe that you would fall for all the crap in this song

I want you
And only you and only you, my love

Live In Las Vegas

We were the cream of the crop
We were the pick of the pack
We were as big as they come
We said we'd never look back
We were financially fine
And we were critically cool
And we were larger than life
And we could break any rule
And that's the way that it was
The way that it was

We said it's all like a dream
Another glass of champagne
I said, "Well, you haven't changed"
You're just a little more vain
And we could laugh till we cried
About how easy it was
And we could do anything
And be accepted because
That's just the way that it is
The way that it is

I was on the cutting edge
And you were so sharp
We were like two angels
With a custom built harp
Now we're in Nevada
And we're nothing at all
Now we're in Nevada
And it's after the fall

And we're live in Las Vegas
Saturday night
Live in Las Vegas
Every night
Put your hands together
Welcome them
Live in Las Vegas

I got so used to the lights
And now I'm here in the dark
I got so used to the caviar
And now there are sharks
We do whatever they want
But they don't know what they want
They just keep ordering drinks
And yelling, "Hey, you get off"
And that's the way that it is
The way that it is

I was on the cutting edge
And you were so sharp
We were like two angels
With a custom built harp
Now we're in Nevada
And we're nothing at all
Now we're in Nevada
And it's after the fall

And we're live in Las Vegas
Saturday night
Live in Las Vegas
Every night
Put your hands together

Welcome them
Live in Las Vegas

We were the cream of the crop
We were the pick of the pack
We were as big as they come
We said we'd never look back
But now we are looking back
A couple lifetimes ago
Around the poker and blackjack
And now on with the show
And that's the way that it is
The way that it is

Live in Las Vegas
Saturday night
Live in Las Vegas
Every night
Put your hands together
Welcome them
Live in Las Vegas

Vegas... Vegas... Vegas...

Lighten Up, Morrissey

She won't go out with me, no she won't go out
'Cause my intellect's paper thin
She won't go out with me, no she won't go out
Since my intellect's not like him

So lighten up, Morrissey

She won't hang out with me, no she won't hang out
'Till my biting wit bites like his
She won't hang out with me, no she won't hang out
'Till my quick retort's quick as his

So lighten up, Morrissey
Lighten up, lighten up
Lighten up, lighten up
Lighten up, Morrissey

She won't have sex with me, no she won't have sex
'Less it's done with a pseudonym
She won't do sport with me, no she won't do sport
Says it's way, way too masculine, look at him

So lighten up, Morrissey
Lighten up, lighten up
Lighten up, lighten up
Lighten up, Morrissey

I got comparisons coming out my ears
And she never can hit the pause
If only Morrissey weren't so Morrissey-esque
She might overlook all my flaws

So lighten up, Morrissey
Lighten up, lighten up
Lighten up, lighten up
Lighten up, Morrissey

She won't dine out with me, no she won't dine out
Says my T-bone steak is at fault
She won't dine out with me, no she won't dine out
With a murderer, pass the salt

Lighten up, lighten up
Lighten up, Morrissey

Here Comes Bob

When I spot a driver worth a second glance
Foot to floorboard, impact soon achieved
Here comes Bob
I ain't subtle in my ways of making friends

Girl, this rubbled mess was caused by my neglect
Of course I'll pay, and by the way, my dear
Here comes Bob
I ain't subtle in my ways of making friends

But here comes Bob
Sometimes I will stoop to hitting two-door coupes
without the frills
But that is just for casual acquaintances,
for stripped-down thrills
Your car, girl, or mine it doesn't matter, doesn't matter no
But for affairs with staying power I go after limousines
It's always nice when something big is acting
as your go-between
For a group encounter I'll hit busses, mobile homes,
or trains to Pittsburgh, Pennsylvania

It's hard to make acquaintances in our big town
Most eyes stare at nothing much at all
But here comes Bob
I ain't subtle in my ways of making friends,
friends, acquaintances

Instant adulation comes to some at birth
Born to queens or corporate entities
But here comes Bob

Bob was 3 years old when he was born
2 years from conception to the birth of Bob
Some things just take longer to arrive
Here Comes Bob
Bob was a celebrity when he arrived

Bobby's parents had no trouble cashing in [they made blade]
All the motion picture people smiled [All the movie people]
Here Comes Bob
Catchy name for widescreen version of the same

INSTRU
Here Comes Bob
All the world was with him & they loved him really loved him & ...

Soon the disenchantment entered this new craze
Bob could not be blamed, he was but three
Here Comes Bob
Such a hollow ring, it now don't mean a thing

Were he born as you or I he'd be content
The novelty is gone, but Bob remains
Here Comes Bob
Home from office to an undemanding wife

At some time we all seek out the Grand Design
Don't ask Bob 'cause he ain't got a hint

Here Comes Bob

Someday they'll put me away
I'll think back on active days
Most were worth the minor scars
Some were worth the damaged cars
And the judge will say to me,
"Bob, you've got a bad means to a worthwhile end"

An end

Well, here comes Bob.

Propaganda

"Hello soldier boy"
Oh boy, she's spewing out her
Propaganda, propaganda

Might makes right, though you are wrong,
You're right to fight her
Propaganda, propaganda, propaganda

"Come to our side," she does say
"Come on over," she does say

Well, I don't need more
Competition for
Her affection
You should fight on
Fight on
Over there

Under The Table With Her

Nobody misses diminutive offspring
Not when there's big wigs there, there
Dinner for twelve is now dinner for ten
'Cause I'm under the table with her

I gave a yelp and they throw me a cutlet
Somebody pats her hair, hair
Everyone's nice to the subhuman species
I'm under the table with her

People all around the world are having
only rice and tea
Two of them should come and take the place
of Laura Lee and Me

(She Got Me) Pregnant

Pregnant
  She got me pregnant
Done using me
I'm just a memory

You know how these girls can be,
they treat you all so casually
They wine you and they dine you,
and expect a little la-dee-dee
And then you learn that though
she's several thousand miles away
There is a part of her she's given you,
and now you have to deal with being

Pregnant
She got me pregnant
She got me pregnant
She got me pregnant
Done using me
I'm just a memory

You know how society is showing some sobriety
By letting individuals decide on how they get their thrills
And if there is a consequence then you are left to deal with it
Government will not be there to tell you what to do if you get

Pregnant
She got me pregnant
She got me pregnant
She got me pregnant
Done using me
I'm just a memory

PREGNANT

Made it in Miami with a Mai Tai in my system
and the promise of a love forever and

Friends are all accusing me of making all
this up that it's a weak attempt at
role reversal and they've heard enough but
I assure them that my morning sickness will
not go away and that ~~I'm thinking of the perfect name~~ an ice cream and a
pickle is the only thing I crave because I'm
for someone who will
a baby shower

Dr McGee said it was twins ~~for~~ me

Maybe you are thinking that a

I'm a middle western

I don't need to tell you of the dangers of a
small ~~town boy~~ country boy who lands in
smack in the middle of a major urban city
and proceeds to sample this and that and
with no apparent consequence until a loaded lady
with a

(She Got Me) Pregnant

Pregnant
She got me pregnant
She got me pregnant
She got me pregnant
How can it be
Acted responsibly

I offer you, I offer you a simple word of warning
Think it's never gonna happen to you, better, better,
better think again

Pregnant
She got me pregnant
She got me pregnant
Done using me
I'm just a memory

Pregnant
She got me pregnant
She got me pregnant
She got me pregnant
How can it be
Acted responsibly

A wham and bam and thank you sir
is all that I would get from her
I never should have given in,
I never should have given her
The golden opportunity to love me and to leave me
Without giving me the time of day
and she is half the world away

I'm pregnant
She got me pregnant
She got me pregnant

She got me pregnant
Done using me
I'm just a memory

Pregnant
She got me pregnant
She got me pregnant
She got me pregnant
How can it be
Acted responsibly

Pregnant
She got me pregnant
Done using me
I'm just a memory

Tryouts For The Human Race

We're just gleams in lover's eyes,
  steam on sweaty bodies in the night
One of us might make it through,
  all the rest will disappear like dew
Pressure building, gettin' hot, give it,
  give it, give it all you've got
When that love explosion comes, my,
  oh my, we want to be someone

Tryouts for the human race,
  from Burlington to Bonn
Ah, we are a quarter billion strong
Tryouts for the human race,
  from twilight time 'til dawn
We just want to be someone

We're the future and the past,
  we're the only way you're gonna last
We're just pawns in a funny game,
  tiny actors in the oldest play
It's an angry sea we face,
  just to get the chance to join the race
Gotta make it, gotta try,
  gotta get the chance to live and die

Tryouts for the human race,
  from Burlington to Bonn
Ah, we are a quarter billion strong
Tryouts for the human race,

from twilight time 'til dawn
We just want to be someone

We must, we must, we must,
we must leave from here
We must, we must, we must,
we must leave from here
Gotta make our play, gotta get away
Gotta make our play, gotta get away
Gotta make our play, gotta get away
Gotta make our play

Let us out of here, let us out of here
Let us out of here, let us out of here

We just want to feel the sun,
be your little daughter or your son
We're just words that lovers use,
words that light that automatic fuse
When that love explosion comes,
my, oh my, we want to be someone

Tryouts for the human race,
from Burlington to Bonn
Ah, we are a quarter billion strong
Tryouts for the human race,
from twilight time 'til dawn
We just want to be someone

Anyone.

My Baby's Taking Me Home

Home, my baby's taking me home
My baby's taking me home
My baby's taking me home

Home, my baby's taking me home
My baby's taking me home
My baby's taking me home

My baby's taking me home
My baby's taking me home
My baby's taking me home
My baby's taking me home

My baby's taking me home
My baby's taking me home
My baby's taking me home
My baby's taking me home

As we walk through the morning rain
And the skies are clearing
And the streets are glistening
Streets named for New England trees
A rainbow forms
But we're both colorblind
But we can hear what others can't hear
We can hear the sound of a chorus singing

Home, my baby's taking me home
My baby's taking me home
My baby's taking me home
My baby's taking me home
My baby's taking me home

My baby's taking me home
My baby's taking me home
My baby's taking me home
My baby's taking me home

My baby's taking me home
My baby's taking me home
My baby's taking me home
My baby's taking me home

When I'm With You

When I'm with you
     I never have a problem when I'm with you
I'm really well-adjusted when I'm with you, with you, with you
When I'm with you

When I'm with you
I lose a lot of sleep when I'm with you
I meet a lot of people when I'm with you, with you, with you
When I'm with you

It's the break in the song
When I should say something special
But the pressure is on and I can't make up nothing special
Not when I'm with you

When I'm with you
I never feel like garbage when I'm with you
I almost feel normal when I'm with you, with you, with you
When I'm with you

When I'm with you
I'm always hot and bothered when I'm with you
I always need a shower when I'm with you, with you, with you
When I'm with you

It's that break in the song
When I should say something special
But the pressure is on and I can't make up nothing special
Not when I'm with you

When I'm with you
I never need a mirror when I'm with you
I don't care what I look like when I'm with you,
with you, with you
When I'm with you

When I'm with you
I never have a problem when I'm with you
I'm really well-adjusted when I'm with you
I lose a lot of sleep when I'm with you
I meet a lot of people when I'm with you
I never feel like garbage when I'm with you
I almost feel normal when I'm with, with you, with you
When I'm with you

I've Never Been High

Thrill rides and places, wide-open spaces
 Played in a band, such harmless novelties
Where's the forgetting, where's the regretting
Of lurid acts that never came to be

I've never been high, never been high, never been high
I've never been high, never been high, never been high

If I could buy it, maybe I'd try it
But my connections aren't what they once were
Paint me a picture, read me some scripture
Maybe I should've stuck it out with her

I've never been high, never been high, never been high
I've never, I've never, I've never been high
I've never been high, never been high, never been high

I've celebrated, birthdays and waited
Waited and waited, tomorrow's just a tease
Then I'll be something, then I'll be something
Look there's a camera, smile and say cheese

I've never, I've never, I've never been high
I've never been high, never been high, never been high

Pretending To Be Drunk

That is what I had intended, pretending to be drunk
A little change in character, I'm pretending to be drunk
You think I am weak and feeble
You think I'm a bore
When you drag me to a party
Soon I'm out the door
Next time I'll portray a suave sophisticated hunk
That is what I had intended, pretending to be drunk

That is what I had intended, pretending to be drunk
A bit of "I have lived and loved," I'm pretending to be drunk
You say I could use some swagger
You say toughen up
I am rigid as a board
You tell me loosen up
I'm so loose and I'm so tough
That I can barely move
That is what I had intended, pretending to be drunk

You notice a transformation, pretending to be drunk
I've lost all my inhibitions, pretending to be drunk
You can take me to the soiree
And be proud of me
Everyone will be impressed
I'll pass out on your knee
Now I am so continental, they think that it's nice
Think I'll pretend to be drunk for the rest of my life

That is what I had intended, pretending to be drunk

Equator

I always felt that I had quite a gift as a judge of
human character
This is the day and the time and the place
and I wonder, wonder where you are
Surely, we set it for 3 pm
Surely, we said it was March the 10th

(Equator, Equator)
You said you'd meet there
You must be just around the bend

All of the gifts are now melted or dead,
and I'm, sorry, sorry in advance
I'll make it up to you, that I can promise you,
if I am given just half the chance
God, you'll be laughing, I look a mess
But you see I've been half way around this place
(Equator, Equator)
You said you'd meet me there
(Equator, Equator)
You said you'd be right there
(Equator, Equator)
Oh yeah

(Equator, Equator)
You said you'd meet there
You must be just around the bend

I've got to stop here and rest for a moment,
I'm sure that you're not far away
You always walked just as slow as you talked,
letting me think I could have my way
I wasn't fooled for a second, girl
I knew it was you who controlled our world
(Equator, Equator)
You said you'd meet me there
(Equator, Equator)
You said you'd be right there
(Equator, Equator)
Oh yeah

Tits

Harry, it's good of you to stay
Hear every word I say
And not just duck away

God, these drinks are something warm and watered down
Barkeep, how 'bout some ice
Hey, Harry sit back down
Say, that little thing there's fine from behind

They all look good after three or four
So drink Harry, drink Harry, drink 'til you can't
see no more
Of anything, no more of anything
Drink Harry, drink Harry, drink 'til you can't see no more

For months, for years,
Tits were once a source of fun and games at home
And now she says, tits are only there to feed our little Joe
So that he'll grow

Harry, it's really rough at home
I've caught her on the phone
Hey, who's that on the phone?
Oh, that's no one dear,
The standard sort of line
Harry, you know me well,
You know that I'm not blind
Hey, you ain't been drinking
Don't you know I'm buying?

They all taste good after three or four
So drink Harry, drink Harry, drink 'til you can't
drink no more

Of anything, no more of anything
Drink Harry, drink 'til you can't drink no more

How well I know
Tits were once a source of fun and games at home
And now she says, tits are only there to feed our
little Joe
So that he'll grow

God, the room is spinning round
Hey, drive me home old pal
God, you sure get around
Harry, I know it's you who's breaking up my home
Harry, don't say a word, just drop me off at home
Harry, forgive me Harry, let's have just one more

It's all so good after three or four
It's all so good after three or four
It's all so good after three or four

So let's drink Harry, drink 'til we can't drink no more
Of anything, no more of anything
Drink Harry, drink Harry, drink 'til we can't drink no more

How well I know
Tits were once a source of fun and games at home
And now she says, tits are only there to feed our
little Joe
So that he'll grow into a man

So let's drink Harry, drink 'til we can't see no more

Ugly Guys With Beautiful Girls

Ugly guys with beautiful girls
You always know what the story is
Beautiful girls with ugly guys
What do they take us for anyway?

Ugly guys with beautiful girls
Ugly guys with beautiful girls

As they walk down the street arm in arm
I see them
And once again feel the need to ask myself the question
The question that has weighed heavily on me of late
How is it possible that a guy and a girl
so dissimilar in physical appearance,
there being such a disparity in how attractive each is,
be nonetheless in what would appear to be a relationship?

It ain't done with smoke and mirrors
It ain't done with smoke and mirrors
It ain't done with smoke and mirrors
Ugly guys with beautiful girls
Ugly guys with beautiful girls
Ugly guys with beautiful girls

How do we explain this?
An attraction of opposites?
No, that theory has been refuted
by many experts in the fields of human psychology
A much greater attraction seems to come
from one more similar to oneself
Personality perhaps?

~~I see the couple walking down the street arm in~~ ~~to~~

~~Do you see the couple walking down the street arm in arm? Yes, then~~

~~I see them and once again feel~~

~~I see them as well and once again feel the need~~
~~the couple walking arm in arm approaches in~~

As they walk down the street arm in arm, I
see them and ~~who~~ ~~yourself~~ once again feel the need
to ask myself the question, the question that has
weighed heavily on me of late. How is it possible
that a guy and a girl so dissimilar in physical
appearance, ~~one unattractive at best, the other extremely~~ how
~~attractive each is~~ there being such a disparity in ~~any~~
~~eyes being his and her respective attractiveness~~,
be nonetheless in what would appear to be some sort
of relationship.

How do we explain this?
An attraction of opposites? No, that theory has been
refuted by many experts in the fields of human psychology.
A much greater attraction seems to come from one
more similar to oneself.

Personality, perhaps? Without intending to sound
judgmental, I would say that he doesn't ~~appear~~ look
like what was once called a "live wire" or "the
life of the party." He appears rather expressionless. His
movements are still and, even, awkward.

Perhaps he is a person of some intellect — an expert in
science, the arts, political theory. No, I think not.
See how well tailored his clothes are, how well cut his
hair is.

Ugly Guys WIth Beautiful Girls

137

Without intending to sound judgmental
I would say that he doesn't look like
what was once called "live wire" or "the life
of the party"
He appears rather expressionless
His movements are stiff and even awkward
Perhaps he's a person of some intellect,
an expert in science,
the arts, political theory?
No, I think not.
See how well tailored his clothes are
How well cut his hair is

It ain't done with smoke and mirrors
It ain't done with smoke and mirrors
It ain't done with smoke and mirrors
Ugly guys with beautiful girls
Ugly guys with beautiful girls
Ugly guys with beautiful girls

I must confess to you, my listeners
that I have been a little less than honest
in pretending I had no answers to my
previous questions
You see, I lost someone very dear to me
someone very beautiful
to someone much like him
Ah, you ask, surely there must have been
other areas where you were deficient and he was not
No, I don't believe so.
My shortcomings were of an economic nature
He was rich, I was not
You see, I underestimated the appeal to her of things

Imported thing on wheels
Large things with manicured lawns and
Olympic swimming pools
Things to wear around her neck that would
glisten in the night light
Things!

Still I am not bitter
Rather, I am an observer
Who saw firsthand how life may not be fair
Would things have turned out differently
between me and her
Had I moved up the corporate ladder quicker
Been born of more noble stock
Or done better on one of our journeys to Las Vegas?

Perhaps.
In fact, I am certain of it.
Things would have tuned out differently
between me and her
I know this now
It ain't done with smoke and mirrors

It ain't done with smoke and mirrors
Ugly guys with beautiful girls

Ugly guys with beautiful girls
You always know what the story is

I Married A Martian

Well, I married a Martian
And boy, am I sorry

Well, she came down from the sky
She couldn't stand the attitude there
She took human form, not bad
She seemed different
She had a European flair
And I said, "Where you from?"
And she said, she said, "I'm from Mars"

I married a Martian
Her loving is different
Viva la difference
Every, every night

I married a Martian
I took her to Vegas
I dressed her in ermine
She had the time of her life

Though she called me Mister Right
I could sense something was wrong
She was hardly home at all
She'd keep telling me
She was doing studies of Earth
She had tendencies to flirt
And it really did hurt me

I married a Martian
Boy, am I sorry
I don't recommend it
To anyone in their right mind

I married a Martian
I think I see changes
I know I see changes
She doesn't look like our kind

Her arms, her legs
Were growing, and growing
Her form, once thin
Was changing, was changing
I can't describe
The changes, so gruesome
She looked, she seemed
So Martian

I married a Martian
I'm going to Vegas
It isn't for pleasure
I'm getting a quickie divorce

I married a Martian
And boy, am I sorry
I don't recommend it
To anyone in their right mind

I married a Martian
Who was I kidding
She only had loved me

'Cause I was the first guy she saw

I married a Martian
And now it is over
Go back to your cronies
Back to your own form of life

I married a Martian
They're good in the movies
Dramatic potential
But they're not so hot in real life

I Wish I Looked A Little Better

Turn out the light, yeah, the light
And I might have a chance
I guess I look slightly worse
Than the Elephant Man
Whoa, oh, oh, I wish I looked a little better
Whoa, oh, oh, I wish I looked a little better

I went to high school
And majored in looking real bad
I got a real ugly mom
And a real ugly dad
Whoa, oh, oh, I wish I looked a little better
Whoa, oh, oh, I wish I looked a little better

Dress for success
That's what they say
I'm such a mess
That there just ain't no way

I know my breath is the sweetest
It really is great
But when I try just to kiss you
You say, "Better wait"
Whoa, oh, oh, I wish I looked a little better
Whoa, oh, oh, I wish I looked a little better

Dress for success
That's what they said
Gimme some clothes
To slap over my head

Whoa, oh, oh, I wish I looked a little better
Whoa, oh, oh, I wish I looked a little better

I went to Balboa Island
And laid in the sand
I may be ugly as sin
But at least now I'm tan
Whoa, oh, oh, I wish I looked a little better

Whoa, oh, oh, I wish I looked a little better

Shopping Mall Of Love

I found my thrill
I found my thrill
I found my thrill in Beverly Hills

Folks call her Jill
Folks call her Jill
Folks call her Jill but that ain't what I call her

She's like a star
She's like a star
She's like a star in a long running TV series

And we make love
And we make love
And we make love all the time

Come
The shopping mall of love
All for free
The shopping mall of love
Quality
The shopping mall of love
All for free
The shopping mall of love

She makes me laugh
She makes me laugh
She makes me laugh

Come
The shopping mall of love
All for free

The shopping mall of love
Quality
The shopping mall of love
All for free
The shopping mall of love

She's so uninhibited
She's so unlimited
That's just the start

She's so magnificent
She's so significant
A work of art

Like the Mona Lisa
Venus de Milo
Or the Pieta
Or a Reclining Nude On The Wall

I found my thrill
I found my thrill
I found my thrill in Beverly Hills

The Toughest Girl In Town

She won't marry you
She don't look good in white
Don't try sweet talk
Unless you're hot for a fight
Still there's something that
Drives the guys half-insane
Ain't they heard that their love
For her is in vain

And all the guys in town
Just love to hang around
The toughest girl in town

Look outside and you'll see
The rain pouring down
That's the sign that
She's now on your side of town
Plan your life around
Someone proper and clean
That's the smart thing
But that means nothing to me

And all the guys in town
Just love to hang around
The toughest girl in town

She's not evil
She's just a little confused

All her life she's been
Set upon and abused
Given that, she's more interesting
Than the rest
Given that, she's the one
Who I love the best

Like all the guys in town
I love to hang around
The toughest girl in town

How To Get Your Ass Kicked

Look askance
Just a glance
Just enough
To incite the wrath
Of her confidante
Strong though gaunt

And that's how to get your ass kicked
How to get your ass kicked

Never learn
To discern
Areas
Where you don't belong
So you venture out
Head in clouds

And that's how to get your ass kicked
How to get your ass kicked

I know, I know, I know, I know

Driving home
Bikes in chrome
Cut you off
And you flip them off
And they take their turns
Many turns

And that's how to get your ass kicked
How to get your kicked

I know, I know, I know, I know

In the end
Then is when
You will pray
But you won't be answered
And then you'll go
End of show

And that's how to get your ass kicked
How to get your ass kicked

Oh well, oh well, oh well, oh well

This Town Ain't Big Enough
For Both Of Us

Zoo time is she and you time
The mammals are your favorite type,
and you want her tonight
Heartbeat, increasing heartbeat
You hear the thunder of stampeding rhinos,
elephants and tacky tigers
This town ain't big enough for the both of us
And it ain't me who's gonna leave

Flying, domestic flying
And when the stewardess is near
do not show any fear
Heartbeat, increasing heartbeat
You are a khaki-colored bombardier,
it's Hiroshima that you're nearing
This town ain't big enough for both of us
And it ain't me who's gonna leave

Daily, except for Sunday
You dawdle in to the café
where you meet her each day
Heartbeat, increasing heartbeat
As twenty cannibals have hold of you,
they need their protein just like you do
This town ain't big enough for the both of us
And it ain't me who's gonna leave

Shower, another shower
You've got to look your best for her
and be clean everywhere

Heartbeat, increasing heartbeat
The rain is pouring on the foreign town,
the bullets cannot cut you down
This town ain't big enough for the both of us
And it ain't me who's gonna leave

Census, the latest census
There'll be more girls who live in town
though not enough to go round
Heartbeat, increasing heartbeat
You know that this town isn't big enough,
not big enough for both of us
This town isn't big enough,
not big enough for both of us
And I ain't gonna leave

Strange Animal

When the strange animal with the strange set of plans
    Came to town last July, there was blood on his hands
And it now comes to light, he had been in a fight
With some government men who were high as a kite

What a strange animal we are

There are songs that are sealed that will not let you in
But he came upon a song that was open to him
To get out of the rain, it was cold, it was strong
Well, the strange animal walked right into the song

What a strange animal we are
What a strange, what a strange animal
What a strange animal we are

"I had nowhere to go, so I entered your song
 So I entered your song, hope you don't think me wrong
 Well, it's warm and it's dry, it's a nasty old night
 It's a nasty old night and I must look a sight"

There's something 'bout him that is frightening
And right on cue, a bolt of lightning

"I'll just sit over here till the chorus appears
 Would you think it a sin, if I start chiming in?"

What a strange animal we are
We are
What a strange animal we are

"If I may be quite frank, and I'm not pulling rank
 And I know I'm a guest, and I know you know best

But this song lacks a heart, comes off overly smart
An emotional core, ain't that what songs are for?"

There's something 'bout him I'm not liking
Somebody to tell him to get hiking

"But you need to be clear and a lot more sincere
Wake me up, will you friend, when the verse finally ends?"

What a strange animal we are
We are

But the ones in the song who had been there so long
Grew impatient and seethed and they asked him to leave
But he said,
"Not so fast, unaware of my past
You allowed me inside, you can't push me aside
When the song lets me in, I can see where it's been
If it's broken some hearts, if it's been in the charts
But this song shows no signs of a grander design
Entertainment or art, one should know from the start"

"You're in need of a fix, or a totally remix
So I must kill you all, start again, had a ball
I'm a strange animal and I find you quite dull
Here's that chorus again, that can stay, here's the end"

What a strange animal we are

Mickey Mouse

Can you raise both your hands and clap 'em
Can you say, "Sure, I'll always try"
Can you make friends among people and animals
Basically, everything is easy
Give it a try, you'll see I'm right
'Cause if a mouse can be special, well so can you

And my name is Mickey Mouse
To my right is Minnie Mouse
And we own a little place in Disneyland, California

Let's have a party and be happy
Can we invite my closest friends
We can ask Donald Duck, Pluto, and all the gang

And my name is Mickey Mouse
To my right is Minnie Mouse
And we own a little place in Disneyland, California

Well, you should try to smile, dear
Get yourself a pet, deer
Dog
Cat
Bird
Pig
Lamb
Horse
Cow
Fox

Wolf
Snake
Ox
Fish
A goldfish
Mouse

And my name is Mickey Mouse
To my right is Minnie Mouse
And we own a little place in Disneyland,
California

Did you raise both your hands and clap 'em
Did you say, "Sure, I'll always try"
'Cause you look hesitant, wary, or am I
wrong
You can go off and be a loner
Maybe you can't believe a mouse
But when you feel the need, come back
I'm here...for...you...and you

And my name is Mickey Mouse
To my right is Minnie Mouse
And we own a little place in Disneyland,
California

Let's Go Surfing

Rain is pouring down
In our land-locked town
Skies are always gray
Let's go surfing, babe
Somewhere there is hope
Somewhere there are dreams
Far from soot and smoke
Let's go surfing, babe

Tonight as we look at the moon and the stars
From our room with security bars
There's a westerly wind that is blowing
both our minds and
Both our feet walk through sand that's as white
as the snow
Past the people named Kelley and Joe
Who have nothing in common with anyone we
know, we know they're

Too Wagnerian
Too Shakespearian
Too impossible
Let's go surfing, babe
Somewhere there is hope
Far from everything
Far from misanthropes
Let's go surfing, babe

Tonight, from a room only Dickens could love
Wearing moth-eaten sweaters and gloves
We will open the window and feel an on-shore
wind a-blowing in

Rain is pouring down
In our land-locked town
Skies are always gray
Let's go Surfing, babe

Somewhere there is hope   Far from everything
Somewhere there are dreams
(Far from soot and smoke)   Far from misanthropes
Let's Go Surfing, babe
Tonite, as we look at the moon and the stars
From our room with security bars
there's a westerly wind that is blowing both our minds and
Both our feet walk through sand that's as white as the snow
Past the people named Kelley and Abe
who have nothing in common with anyone we know
we know | they're   we've ever known

Too Wagnerian   Town
Too Shakespearian   From a room only Dickens could love
Too unbearable   Wearing overcoats, scarves and
Let's Go Surfing, babe   wool gloves
                             We hear shattering glass as on
                             on shore is blowing the
                             the street and it's here
                             and we're paddling hard as we can
                             half a mile from the heat of the sand
                             then we turn and we catch a
                             the perfect wave wave
                                    the perfect wave

Let's Go Surfing

Grab our boards from the back of our van
Paddle out 'til we can't see the sand
Spin around and drop into the wave we hope
will never end

Somewhere there is hope
Somewhere there are dreams
Far from everything
Let's go surfing, babe

Tonight, grab our boards from the back of our van
Paddle out 'til we can't see the sand
Spin around and drop into the wave we hope
will never end

Catch a wave, a wave, a wave
Catch a wave, a wave, a wave

Somewhere there is hope
Somewhere there are dreams
Far from everything

Let's go surfing, babe

Let The Monkey Drive

We're driving north on Highway 1
Toward Santa Barbara, lots of sun
Pacific Ocean on our left hand side
Though Santa Barbara's on our mind,
Our love can't wait till after 9
So she says, "Can't we let the monkey drive?"

Let the monkey drive
We can have our fun
As we hop in back
Out on Highway 1
Let him take the wheel
'Neath the setting sun
Let the monkey drive
Out on Highway 1

He's passing cars and passing trucks,
and swigs some coffee from Starbucks
And in the backseat everything is fine
He never pries in our affairs,
he never listens, never stares
And we three are enjoying our long ride

Let the monkey drive
We can have our fun
As we hop in back
Out on Highway 1
Let him take the wheel
'Neath the setting sun
Let the monkey drive
Out on Highway 1

Let the monkey drive
And it's only fair
It's the monkey's car
And he hates to share
Let him chauffeur us
While we have our fun
Keep our love alive
Out on Highway 1

With obscene gestures learned from me
He works off some hostility
Toward drivers who might cut him off or slide
I think his license has expired
He seems to be a little wired
He has some trouble staying on our side

But you and me are doing fine
We couldn't wait till after 9
Impossible, our love is way too strong
He hits the brakes a couple times
But everything is superfine
I'm glad the monkey asked to come along

Let the monkey drive
We can have our fun
As we hop in back
Out on Highway 1
Let him take the wheel
'Neath the setting sun
Let the monkey drive
Out on Highway 1

Let the monkey drive
And it's only fair
It's the monkey's car
And he hates to share
Let him chauffeur us
While we have our fun
Keep our love alive
Out on Highway 1

Let the monkey drive
We can have our fun
As we hop in back
Out on Highway 1
Let him take the wheel
'Neath the setting sun
Let the monkey drive
Out on Highway 1

Let the monkey drive
And it's only fair
It's the monkey's car
And he hates to share
Let him chauffeur us
While we have our fun
Keep our love alive
Out on Highway 1

A Walk Down Memory Lane

We all expected champagne
But it never did come
But it never did come
We said, "Hey, where's our champagne?"
And they gave us a gun
Said to go and have fun
So many riches just out of reach
Coming attractions washed up on the beach, oh yeah

Let's take a walk
A walk down memory lane
Past the signs of the times
That lit our little way
And decide what it is
That made it all this way
And decide who it is
That might make it O.K.

The sun bears down on the man
With a girl on his arm
She's a victim of charm
She thinks, Sinatra the man
Think of him as you walk
Think of him as you talk
So many riches just out of reach
Coming attractions washed up on the beach, oh yeah

Let's take a walk
A walk down memory lane
Past the signs of the times
That lit our little way
And decide what it is
That made it all this way

And decide who it is
That might make it O.K.

They say in 10 million years
That the sun'll burn out
And that'll be that
She drinks a couple of beers
Takes a look at the sun
She would love to see that
So many riches just out of reach
Coming attractions washed up on the beach, oh yeah

Let's take a walk
A walk down memory lane
Past the signs of the times
That lit our little way
And decide what it is
That made it all this way
And decide who it is
That might make it O.K.

Miss The Start,
Miss The End

Neither has a predilection, neither has an afterthought
And neither chair gets warm at all
And neither takes their jacket off
For this they'll pay the same money to see the event
As you and I and we'll see it all

They've never seen a curtain rise, a kick-off or the final gun
And never have they seen the titles
Flashing cross the rising sun
I'm done, I'm done, I'm done, I will be silent again
Quiet now, it's all gonna begin

Miss the start, miss the end
'Cause they're such very good friends
And there are things to be loved and things to only attend
Miss the start, miss the end

The opening bars and the closing bars might as well not exist
They're not needed, needed, really needed
You and I have got to see the start
You and I have got to see the end
We need more than just each other
So much more than just each other
They don't need more than each other
Not much more than just each other

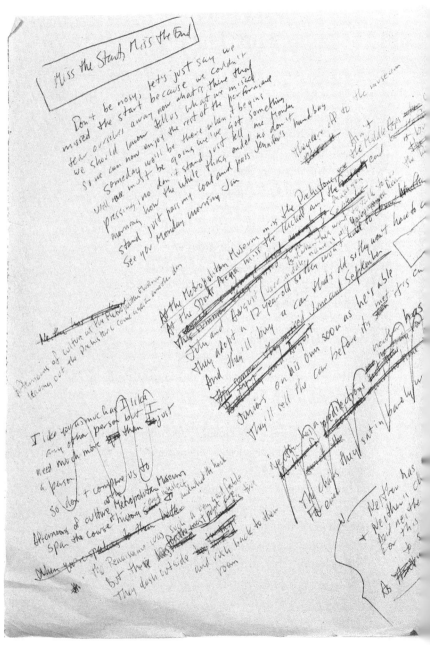

Miss The Start, Miss The End

Miss the start, miss the end
Cause they're such very good friends
And they can't bear to be
Out of their own private dream
For any more than the minimum

For any more than the minimum
The way they start + ends
their own   a flaw

Miss the Start, Miss the end
Cause they're such very Good
friends
And there are things to be loved
And things to only attend

Miss the start, miss the end

Miss the start, miss the end
Though they try hard to extend
There are things to be loved
and things to only attend
Miss the start, miss the end

Middle

The opening bars and the closing bars
might as well not exist, they're
not needed, needed, really needed
they would rather be in private
they'd miss the start to be) in private
(cause they're)
They miss the moment when the screen
is blank except The End is seen

They missed December to January
They missed   now pronounced
you man and...

Sometimes I don't think that they are
from it all   it seems that
they have always been   she was she she and always
will be as they are
I can't see them passing away
When Gabriel blows his horn   they'll be away

They don't need the total picture, just a drawing of each other
Hung inside their bungalow
Where wondrous things are all discovered
You and I must see how it starts and ends
And tell them what they missed once again

Miss the start, miss the end
'Cause they're such very good friends
And there are things to be loved and things to only attend
Miss the start, miss the end

Bon Voyage

Bon voyage, bon voyage, bon voyage
Clouds forming on the gospel sky,
trouble is about to brew on us
It didn't matter that we tried,
they can only take a few of us
The fins and the paws and hooves and feet,
saunter up the gangway
The randomest sampling is complete,
God, could there be some way

That I could
Wear a hood
Or by the
Way I stood
Sneak aboard with you
Imitate
Imitate
Imitate
Imitate
They still know it's you

Bon voyage, bon voyage, bon voyage,
peace be with all of you
I wish that I, I wish that I,
were one of you

Tears falling on the sloping sand,
they're about to leave and we will stay
All governed by the rules of chance,
they're about to leave and we will stay
Goodbye to my lucky friends and foes,
glad that we could know you

Everyone sends their last hello,
I wish that we could join you

Two of you
Two of them
Two of those
Two of them
Safety for the few
Two of you
Two of them
Two of those
Two of them
They will start anew

Bon voyage, bon voyage, bon voyage,
peace be with all of you
I wish that I, I wish that I, I wish that I?

Bon voyage, bon voyage, bon voyage

Bickering
Dickering
Bickering
Dickering
Everything that moves
Bickering
Dickering
Bickering
Dickering
Final, futile moves

Bon voyage, bon voyage, bon voyage, peace be with all of you
I wish that I, I wish that I, I wish that I?

Bon voyage, bon voyage, bon voyage...

I Thought I Told You
To Wait In The Car

66 "I thought I told you to wait in the car"
   "I thought I told you to wait in the car"

What's she doing now?
Has the encore come yet
And the bravas and bouquets
Don't tell me, don't tell me
Someday I'll find a mind of my own
'Til then, I'm content to hear her say

"I thought I told you to wait in the car"
"I thought I told you to wait in the car"

What's she doing now?
What's she doing now?
What's she doing now?

Autographing autobiographies
Adding to discographies
Don't tell me, don't tell me
There's no such thing as a perfect situation
That's what I say when I hear her scream

"I thought I told you to wait in the car"
"I thought I told you to wait in the car"

I'll turn on the radio
And look at myself in the rearview mirror
I know she has an image to protect
I know she's not just being mean when she screams

"I thought I told you to wait in the car"

What's she doing now?
Meeting leaders of the Free World
She's dressed in black, she's their poster girl
Don't tell me, don't tell me
I know she has an image to protect
I know she's not just being mean when she screams

"I thought I told you to wait in the car"
"I thought I told you to wait in the car"

Just a glimpse of it all
Just a taste of it all
Just one foot in the door
In the door of dreamland
In the door of dreamland

"I thought I told you to wait in the car"

Walking in on an afternoon tryst
Can be a source of embarrassment
Embarrassment for all concerned
Don't tell me, don't tell me
In my wildest dreams
I never thought of Warren Beatty as a rival

"I thought I told you to wait in the car"
"I thought I told you to wait in the car"

I Married Myself

I married myself
I'm very happy together
I married myself
I'm very happy together

I married myself
I'm very happy together
Long, long walks on the beach, lovely times
I married myself, I'm very happy together
Candlelight dinners home, lovely times

I married myself
I'm very happy together
I married myself
I'm very happy together

This time it's gonna last, this time it's gonna last
Forever, forever, forever
This time it's gonna last, this time it's gonna last
Forever, forever, forever

I married myself
I'm very happy together
Long, long walks on the beach, lovely times
I married myself, I'm very happy together
Candlelight dinners home, lovely times

This time it's gonna last, this time it's gonna last
Forever, forever, forever
This time it's gonna last, this time it's gonna last
Forever, forever, forever

Song index:

A

Achoo 53

Aeroflot 71

B

Batteries Not Included 104

Bullet Train 45

Bon Voyage 169

C

Change 75

E

Equator 132

F

Falling In Love With Myself 19

Funny Face 39

G

Girl From Germany 65

Ghost of Liberace, The 37

Gratuitous Sax 78

H

Hear No Evil, See No Evil, Speak No Evil 88

Here Comes Bob 115

High C 21

How Do I Get To Carnegie Hall? 50

How To Get Your Ass Kicked 149

I

I Bought The Mississippi River 61

I Can't Believe You Would Fall For
All The Crap In This Song 109

I Married a Martian 140

I Married Myself 173

In The Future 27

Instant Weight Loss 83

I Thought I Told You To Wait In The Car 171

I've Never Been High 130

I Wish I looked A Little Better 143

L

Let The Monkey Drive 160

Let's Get Funky 34

Let's Go Surfing 157

Lost and Found 73

Lighten Up, Morrissey 113

Live In Las Vegas 110

Looks Aren't Everything 98

Looks, Looks, Looks 105

Louve, The 92

M

Madonna 30

Metaphor 22

Mickey Mouse 155

Miss The Start, Miss The End 165

My Baby's Taking Me Home 126

My Other Voice 85

N

National Crime Awareness Week 86

Nothing To Do 95

Number One Song In Heaven, The 102

O

Over The Summer 100

P

Perfume 47

Photoshop 90

Pineapple 93

Popularity 68

Pretending To Be Drunk 131

Propaganda 118

R

Rhythm Thief, The 77

Rock, Rock, Rock 58

S

(She Got Me) Pregnant 120

Sherlock Holmes 35

Shopping Mall Of Love 145

Sisters 69

Strange Animal 153

Suburban Homeboy 32

T

This is the Renaissance 43

This Town Ain't Big Enough For Both Of Us 151

Those Mysteries 63

Tits 134

Toughest Girl In Town, The 147

Tryouts For The Human Race 124

U

Ugly Guys With Beautiful Girls 136

Under The Table With Her 119

V

Very Next Fight, The 81

W

Walk Down Memory Lane 163

Wedding of Jacqueline Kennedy To Russell Mael, The 97

What Are All These Bands So Angry About? 79

When Do I Get To Sing "My Way" 25

When I Am With You 128

Whippings And Apologies 54

Without Using Hands 56

Υ

Young Girls 41

"Metaphor," "When Do I Get To Sing 'My Way'," "Madonna," "Suburban Homeboy," "Let's Get Funky," "Sherlock Holmes," "The Ghost of Liberace," "Funny Face," "Young Girls," "This is the Renaissance," "Bullet Train," "Perfume," "How Do I Get To Carnegie Hall," "Rock, Rock, Rock," "Those Mysteries," "Popularity," "Girl From Germany," "Sisters, Aeroflot," "Change," "The Rhythm Thief," "Gratuitous Sax," "What Are All Those Bands So Angry About?," "The Very Next Fight," "Instant Weight Loss," "National Crime Awareness Week," "Hear No Evil, See No Evil, Speak No Evil," "Photoshop," "Over The Summer," "I Can't Believe You Would Fall For All The Crap In This Song," "Live in Las Vegas," "Lighten Up, Morrissey," "Here Comes Bob," "(She Got Me) Pregnant," "My Baby's Taking Me Home," "When I 'm With You," "I've Never Been High," "Pretending To Be Drunk," "Ugly Guys With Beautiful Girls," "I Married A Martian," "I Wish I Looked A Little Better," "Shopping Mall Of Love," "The Toughest Girl In Town," "How To Get Your Ass Kicked," "Strange Animal," "Mickey Mouse," "Let The Monkey Drive," "Walk Down Memory Lane," "Let's Go Surfing," "Bon Voyage," "I Thought I Told You To Wait In The Car," "I Married Myself"*(Mael/ Mael) ©Imagem Music*

"Falling In Love With Myself Again," "High C," "Achoo," "Without Using Hands," "I Bought The Mississippi River," " Lost and Found," "The Louvre (French translation by Josee Becker)," "Nothing To Do," "Looks Aren't Everything," "Looks, Looks, Looks," "In The Future," "Batteries Not Included," "Propaganda," "Under The Table With Her," "Whippings And Apologies," "Equator," "Tits," "This Town Ain't Big Enough For Both Of Us," "Miss The Start, Miss The End" *(Ron Mael) ©Imagem Music*

"Pineapple," "The Wedding Of Jacqueline Kennedy To Russell Mael" *(Russell Mael) ©Imagem Music*

"My Other Voice"*(Moroder/Mael/Mael) Lyrics by Ron Mael ©Imagem Music /Warner Chappell North America Limited*

"The Number One Song In Heaven" *(Mael/Moroder/Mael) Lyrics by Ron Mael ©Imagem Music/Warner Chappell North America Limited*

TamTam Books

I Spit On Your Graves by Boris Vian (Vernon Sullivan)

Foam of the Daze by Boris Vian

Autumn in Peking by Boris Vian

The Dead All Have the Same Skin by Boris Vian
(Vernon Sullivan)

To Hell With The Ugly by Boris Vian (Vernon Sullivan)

Red Grass by Boris Vian

Evguénie Sokolov by Serge Gainsbourg

Considerations on the Assassination of Gérard Lebovici
by Guy Debord

Gainsbourg the Biography by Gilles Verlant

In The Words Of Sparks... Selected Lyrics by Ron Mael
& Russell Mael (Sparks) / Introduction by Morrissey

The Death Instinct by Jacques Mesrine

For further information about TamTam titles and authors:

www.tamtambooks.com

www.tamtambooks-tosh.blogspot.com

BOOKS